WITHDRAWN
NDSU

PUBLISHED ON THE FUND ESTABLISHED IN
MEMORY OF GANSON GOODYEAR DEPEW

THE DIARY OF ROGER LOWE

THE DIARY OF ROGER LOWE

of

Ashton-in-Makerfield, Lancashire
1663–74

Edited by
WILLIAM L. SACHSE
B.Litt., Ph.D.

Foreword by
PROFESSOR WALLACE NOTESTEIN

NEW HAVEN
YALE UNIVERSITY PRESS
1938

914.272
L95

DA
670
L2
L6

PRINTED IN GREAT BRITAIN

**TO MY PARENTS
AND NAN**

FOREWORD

WE have had so many diaries and autobiographies of country gentlemen and gentlewomen that it is not hard to reconstruct their daily round of activities at a given time, or to gather something of their outlook upon life and of their attitudes towards their fellows in other classes. About clergymen, too, we know a good deal and something of well-to-do business men in country towns. What we do not know about is the lesser folk in villages. Of servants and farm labourers we have only occasional mentions in the diaries and letters of their superiors. Joseph Lister is the only servant in the seventeenth century whose account of himself I can recall, and there are not many in the centuries following. How such men and women lived, what they feared and hoped, remain in most cases unknown. Sometimes a playwright gives us a clue, occasionally a man from the fields walks unobtrusively into the letters of the lady of the manor. But such instances are rare.

That is why Roger Lowe's record of his daily comings and goings is worth attention. Had we made a midsummer-eve's wish for a diary of a common man, we could not have asked for one better than that of this shopkeeper. He was at the centre of village life. He knew everyone in the country round about and had dealings with most of them.

Moreover, he happened to be a young man who drew others to him and went out to meet them. The farmers and farm labourers came to his shop to buy and stayed to talk. They lured him off with them to their club, the alehouse. They went with him to all the alehouses in the parishes around as well as to the chapels. He was up and down the country. Horses could be borrowed sometimes, and if they were not as fleet as motor-cars to-day, they did get over the ground. When horses were not available Roger and his friends took to their feet and walked seven or eight miles and back again.

The young women seem to have been almost as good walkers, a vigorous lot, who did their full share of the work of the community. But they missed little that was going on. They were not shy, they really knew their worth, and seldom waited on male initiative; apparently they were not expected to do so. Yet they were, so far as I can judge, a fairly well-behaved lot and rarely fell into that frailty common to the housemaids of English diaries. There will be those to doubt this opinion and to read more into Roger's narratives of his episodes with young women than I have done.

We can read more, of another kind. Roger had an amusing way of talking, and his friends liked nothing more than to draw him out. He was willing to oblige, and even with stories against himself. Two of these stories he had embodied in the diary, one about leading a recalcitrant ram and the other about eating hot porridge at the servants' table. These relations are as delightful examples of rollicking peasant humour as are to be found in the plays or prose of the seventeenth century. The makers of source books and anthologies will include them; the students of humour will refer to them.

Nothing is more interesting about Roger than his militant conformity. It is a fashion nowadays to sing low about nonconformity. In some way the notion has been conveyed to the public that everything unlovely and middle-class was connected with puritanism and especially with nonconformity. Yet it is puritanism more than any other one factor that has differentiated the English in character from their Continental neighbours. It is nonconformity that has given them much of their particular quality. Those who would interpret the English should spend less words upon country houses, parish churches, bellringers and cricket—those aspects of Englishry dear to *The Times*—and more upon nonconformity in its many phases. What a lot of English thought and movement is concerned with Quakers and Unitarians and Congregationalists! Who can talk about the English village and leave out the Wesleyan chapel?

Roger's nonconformity was not of the loveliest type. He wished to make the best of this world and the next. His expressive piety was a kind of servility towards that Providence who would, he trusted, facilitate his pursuit of the main chance. He was Anglo-Saxon to the core. From the days of Richard Hakluyt who wished to see the English develop colonies in order to foster trade and spread Christianity to the days of Franklin Roosevelt who mixes social idealism and political tie-ups with the underworlds of the great cities, the Anglo-Saxons have known how to do good to others and to do well by themselves.

Yet the reader cannot but like Roger. His lively personality appears in every paragraph. We are as glad to hear him talk as were the men and women of Ashton. We can understand his anxiety for the end of the funeral and the beginning of the feast. He loved food as much as any—a roast goose by preference. He liked to look across the chapel at pretty wenches and to meet them on the town heath. He was not a Samuel Pepys, he lived in a smaller world, but he was not less human.

WALLACE NOTESTEIN

PREFACE

THE Diary of Roger Lowe is preserved in the Leyland Free Library and Museum, in Hindley, Lancashire. Extracts first appeared in the "Local Gleanings" columns of *The Manchester Courier*, beginning on April 21, 1876, and were reprinted in the first volume of *Local Gleanings Relating to Lancashire and Cheshire*, edited by J. P. Earwaker. In the autumn of 1876 the diary was printed in the antiquarian columns entitled the "Chronicle Scrap Book" in *The Leigh Chronicle*, of Leigh, Lancashire. The following year it was reprinted, with a brief introduction and notes, by the *Chronicle*, as a separate publication. This edition omitted a number of passages, however, which have been included here.

I wish to thank Mr. Herbert H. Smith, Librarian and Secretary of the Leyland Free Library and Museum, and his Committee, for their permission to publish the diary; Professor Wallace Notestein, of Yale University, for introducing me to Roger Lowe; and Mr. John Espey, of Merton College, Oxford, for a memorable trip to Lancashire and eyes quick to detect the editor's errors.

W. L. S.

June 5, 1938.
New Haven.

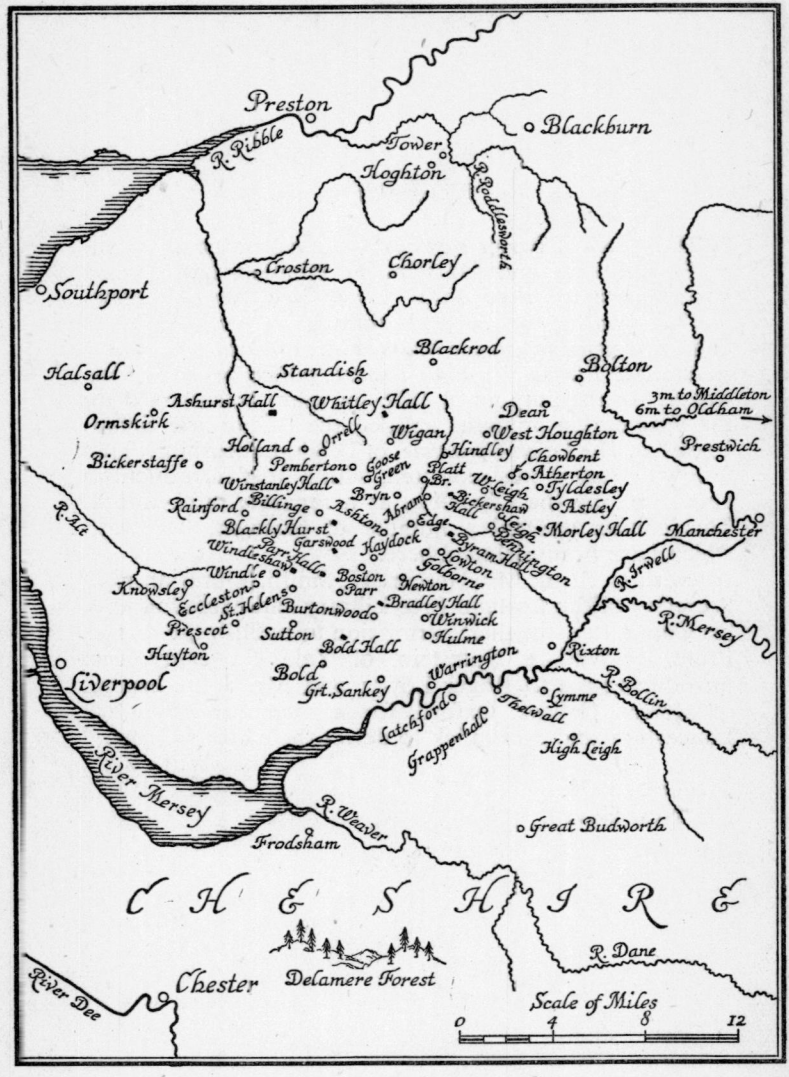

INTRODUCTION

WITH the sole exception of letter-writing, diary-keeping is the single form of literary achievement to which all may attain. We readily grant professional status to the essayist, the novelist, the poet: but who has ever heard of the professional diarist? Every man and woman, of high and low estate, of adventurous or monotonous daily life, has one story to tell, and who can tell it better? "No kind of reading," wrote Macaulay, "is so delightful, so fascinating, as this minute history of a man's self." And for the student of history or of society no document is more revealing. Kept under lock and key by the author, no writing is less influenced by self-consciousness or promoted by self-interest; there is no confessional more secluded.

Unfortunately for students of bygone days the keys to many diaries have been lost forever. Particularly is this true of those kept by persons of humble estate. It is only comparatively recently that Clio, occupied with the annals of kings and war-lords, has considered the butcher and baker and candlestick-maker worthy of her attention. Diarian entries not relating to public events or to persons listed in *Who's Who* have been rigorously blue-pencilled by the most scholarly of editors, and deposited in the waste-baskets of many a publisher. The incentive of preservation is thus gone, and the means, too: for the cottager has no muniment-room or library in which to file his papers with those of his forefathers.

A diary of a seventeenth-century apprentice, such as is presented here, can therefore be regarded as an historical document of considerable rarity and importance. Roger Lowe was an apprentice to a south-Lancashire mercer, a dealer in small wares, and resided in Ashton-in-Maker-

INTRODUCTION

field, a small town of some importance because of its situation midway between Wigan and Warrington. Here, between 1663 and 1674, he kept a diary which fills, in manuscript form, one hundred and fifty closely-written pages. Lowe was not a faithful diarist: his entries are very irregular, and as time goes on the gaps between dates become wider and wider.

What induced Roger Lowe to keep a diary at all? The answer to this question must be conjectural, for Lowe himself offers us no explanation. Different persons keep diaries for different reasons: egotism, addiction to habit, the "itch to record," as Lord Ponsonby calls it, a philosophical urge to survey life, an introspective nature—all these motivations and more must be reckoned with. Lowe lived in a period which Joseph Hunter, in his *Life of Oliver Heywood*, has called "peculiarly the age of diaries." The keeping of diaries, universal as it was to become, cannot be traced in England with any certainty before the sixteenth century; but by the close of the seventeenth courtiers and country gentlemen, clergymen and barristers, soldiers and travellers had all tried their hands at daily autobiography, Pepys and Evelyn had written their classic lines, and diaries were common literary opera.

The chief impetus given to diary-writing in the seventeenth century came from the nonconformists. Puritanical writers of devout manuals advocated the daily recording of thoughts as a means to cultivate a holy life by the discipline of self-examination and self-revelation. Isaac Ambrose, in his *Media: The Middle Things*, first published in 1650, has a section in commendation of diary-keeping, the uses of which he outlines:

"1. Hereby he (the diarist) observes something of God to his soul, and of his soul to God. 2. Upon occasion he pours out his soul to God in prayer accordingly, and either is humbled or thankful. 3. He considers how it is with him in respect of time past, and if he have profited, in grace, to find out the means whereby he hath profited, that he may make more constant use of such means; or wherein he hath decayed, to observe by what temptation he was overcome, that his former errors may make him more wary for the future."*

Now Ambrose's works were extremely popular in Lancashire, where his reputation was considerable. Angier, Newcome, Martindale, Meek, Heywood, and many other nonconformist clergymen practised what they preached and kept journals. And Roger Lowe, a staunch Presbyterian, was very likely influenced by the very passage just cited, for his diary attests his familiarity with the work.

But Roger Lowe's diary is not, fortunately, just a religious exercise. It goes beyond the Puritan and gives us the man. Lowe does not write of events other than those which figure in his daily life and in the lives of those with whom he associates. Living in what had been but a few years before one of the theatres of the Civil Wars, the young apprentice makes but one fleeting reference to the Duke of Hamilton's invasion. A zealous Presbyterian in a time when Church and State were applying legislative screws to the propagators of that faith, Lowe does not once mention the Conventicle Act or the Five-Mile Act, made law even as he wrote. The Dutch War, which extended from 1665 to 1667, is noticed but once—and then because of patriotic services in the local churches. A lone reference is made to the Fire of London, six weeks later, because philanthropical Ashtonians were passing the hat to help the stricken city. The Plague of 1665, the Portuguese marriage of the King, the downfall of Clarendon: all occurred while Lowe diarized, but he used no ink on them. Not once is the recently restored Charles mentioned.

Living far from the national capital and never venturing, so far as we can learn from the diary, beyond the confines of Lancashire and Cheshire, Lowe knew little

* Isaac Ambrose, *Prima, the First Things, in Reference to the Middle and Last Things*, etc. (London, 1674), 118.

and perhaps cared less about national events. He was content to write of births and christenings, of wedding festivities and funeral refreshments, of "trading and how to get wives," of nonconformists' "private days of prayer," of wakes and fairs and ales, of sets of bowling and nights of wooing and visits to neighbouring country-house and manor—in short, to paint a word picture, crude and sketchy in places but drawn from life, of seventeenth-century rural Lancashire. And Lowe, with wide acquaintance, was eminently qualified to do this.

For, humble apprentice though he was, he was a comparatively big fish in the small pond of Ashton. His is a role seldom noticed, because inconspicuous, on the stage of English social history. Historian, ballad-monger, and novelist have, often enough, introduced us to the duarchy of the English village: clergyman and squire, the Church and State of the British countryman. Lowe, raised above his fellow-townsmen and regarded as somewhat of a scholar because of his ability to read, write, and reckon, was the unofficial notary of his rustic community. A hundred clerkly duties devolved upon him in an age when the mother of the Under-Sheriff of Lancashire required his services when she wished to write to her son. The general illiteracy of the time should not be forgotten. A lass wishes to write a love-letter: Lowe acts as amanuensis and will not show it to two curious old codgers in the alehouse. A sick man wishes to make his will: Lowe drafts it "somewhat handsomely." The petty constables are preparing their presentments: Lowe indicts them. Many an apprentice was indentured by Lowe, many an account he reckoned up. Occasionally he is prevailed upon to instruct the young "to endite letters and to cast account up," a task which he seems to accept without enthusiasm. He is recognized universally as a very useful person; he knows all and is known by all, from Mr. Greensworth, the Under-Sheriff, and such local aristocrats as the Byroms and the Gerards, to John Chaddock, his fellow-apprentice.

INTRODUCTION

Although, like Martindale, Lowe seems to have pocketed some recompense for his duties as public secretary, the score was probably more frequently evened by a tankard at the alehouse, and his income from this source amounted to little more than pin-money. To keep body and soul together he tended shop, buying and selling all sorts of small wares for his master. He had been apprenticed—at what age we know not—for nine years. Of his birth and rearing he tells us nothing; his parents, according to the entry of September 13, 1663, both lay buried in the Vicarage Fields in Leigh. His brothers and sisters, occasionally mentioned in the diary, were evidently older than Roger, and had families of their own. Like many other country lads who did not drift to the cities or take to the sea, Lowe may have apprenticed himself as much to find a temporary home as to insure for himself a future livelihood. He does not seem to have wasted any affection on his trade: "I thought it sad," he writes, "for me to be ingagd 9 yeares to stay in Ashton to sell my Master's ware of[f] and get no knowledge." He harps continually on his commercial "greefes," and his unsuccessful career as an independent trader after his graduation from apprenticeship reveals an incompatibility with the life of a shopkeeper.

Lowe's master, although held in considerable respect by the young apprentice, seems to have used him well, and the diary records not a single complaint against him. His identity can only be conjectured. Apprentices' indentures meant a contractual relationship between the master and the apprentice, the former promising meat, drink, and lodging, and often articles of clothing and other necessaries, plus instruction in a trade, and the latter pledging to abide by the regulations laid down by his master—all for a stipulated length of time. These regulations concerned not only the trade which the apprentice was striving to master, but his personal and moral conduct as well. The master was, in theory, the guardian of his apprentice, and it was the master's duty, to quote a

Caroline indenture, "in due and decent manner to chastise and correct him his said servant." Although Lowe's master did not fall short in this particular, the relations between the pair seem to have been ideal. "My Master came to towne," writes Lowe (March 24, 1665), "and he had told me that he had heard many things of me and wishd me for my good to be cautious. He spoke very loveingly to me, and I was efraid before he came, lest he would have beene angry." It is obvious that Roger stood in the good graces of his master's wife, who on one occasion, when equipping him with a new wardrobe, "was so forward as she would have had the tailor left others' worke for to have done my clothes against Sabbath day." His master, moreover, seems to have hearkened to his complaint about his nine-years servitude, for a year later, when Lowe's books showed a profit, he "proffered" him the shop, gave him his freedom, and granted him time in which to pay for the goods on the shelves. Lowe was sorry to leave him, and wrote: "So I was made free; tho I was very sorowfulle, yet my trust is in God."

Lowe's accommodations in the Ashton shop were apparently preferable to living in his master's house, for he calls a summons to come home "sad news." It is easy enough to see why. He enjoyed considerable freedom in Ashton. He was in and out of his shop so much that even Mary Naylor, one of the principal inducements to leave it, was angered at his negligence—"folkes had beene there enquireing for me . . . soe shee was troubled att me." But Roger was young and unmarried (during most of this period, at least) and sociable; he enjoyed good times, and no imported sophistication hindered him from seeking and finding them in Ashton and the neighbouring countryside. Let him who clings to the traditional belief that the Puritan philosophy of life represented the complete negation of everything that is fun spend a day or two with Roger Lowe, bowling for two shillings a set on Golborne Cop, accompanying him to

INTRODUCTION 7

Brynn to see a race, and watching him ride in one from Golborne stocks to Ashton town, witnessing a cock-fight —and solacing his uneasy conscience afterward—hunting foumarts and fishing and robbing magpies' nests. He will discover that many of Roger's evening hours are passed in courting various Lancashire lasses, who seem to have considered him a presentable swain, for they persistently "make much" of him. He will find that the young apprentice did not go to bed with the chickens— and late hours, especially without one's own doors, were a rarity in the seventeenth century, when dark, unpaved country roads made one's safe arrival home a gambling proposition, and candles flickered one to sleep. As far as we can tell from the diary he will not find Lowe dancing or playing cards, but should he lose track of Roger he had better look in the alehouse.

Here Lowe spent nearly as much time as in his shop, and his diary casts a good deal of light on the social functions of the country alehouse. The alehouse of this period, as the public house is to-day, was the poor man's club, and the poor woman's, too, if we may believe the diary. Here villagers and local farmers would gather to "accomodate" one another to a drink or two of ale, the seal of approval, perhaps, on some mutual transaction, or the reward of a victory at bowls, or just a friendly treat to be gossiped over. The frequent resort to alehouses in a Puritan community such as Ashton reminds us that a generation which was to regard moral conduct and abstinence as synonymous had not yet come into being. Nor should we by any means attribute beer-guzzling propensities to those who began the day with drink and a chat at the alehouse, Jefferson cautions us in his *Book about the Table*. The morning draught of ale in the seventeenth century was practically the counterpart of the modern cup of breakfast coffee; the custom bears a close resemblance to the German *zweite Frühstück*. Indeed, the frequent recourse to morning draughts presages a correspondingly consistent moderation on the previous evening, if seventeenth-century constitutions reacted as do those of our own day.

Lowe's visits to the alehouse were not always characterized by such moderation, and many a sickly night and dreary morning are naïvely confessed in the pages of his diary. But it was necessary to be a good fellow. Many a tankard of ale he lays to the exigencies of trade: he had gone to the alehouse because "they ware good customers to me and I durst not but goe for fear of displeasure." As he told the reproachful Reverend Mr. Woods: "I could not trade if att some times I did not spend 2d." But drunkenness and rowdyism revolted him; after a visit to Chester Castle yard he wrote: "The souldiers was most of them all drunke, and glad I was when I was gotten out of the gates from amongst them."

The alehouse as well as the church stood open on Sundays, and Lowe and his companions, including clergymen, patronized them impartially: Ellen Scott and he, we read, "went into Hugh Worthington's and spent 8d; so went into church." On another Sunday he writes: "We ware all afternoone in Ale house. The Lord forgive us." Here, indeed, as in a few other Sunday entries, such as: "This day was not well spent, I must confesse. The Lord humble me for it," we have a hint of Sabbatarian scruples, but they do not seem to have amounted to a deterrent force. We find no mention of Sunday bowling or hunting or horse-racing, it is true, but, besides the alehouse merriment we read of fittings by the tailor, journeys as far afield as to Liverpool and to Chester fair, reckoning of accounts, and sociable intercourse with his friends. For Lowe Sunday was a day when he need not rush back to his counter when a friend tipped him off that his master was in town, a weekly holiday to do with as he would, after he had performed his devotions.

For it was also the "Lord's Day." And for Lowe the regular attendance of religious services was a part of his Puritan training and weekly routine. Church attendance was to him an obligation to God: when he skips a Sunday

INTRODUCTION

he writes: "It was a rainy day, and I was very negligent in my duty to God. The Lord forgive me." His Presbyterian convictions were very real. Because, for instance, he felt that "standing att Gospelle, with other ceremonies now in use, was a meere Romish foperie," he refused to do it, and when reproached declared his intention to betake himself "to such recepticles where I could, to my poor abilitie, serve God without disturbance."

Many a nonconforming clergyman had, in 1662, followed Lowe's example, and of these men we read much in his diary. In 1662 Parliament passed an Act of Uniformity, which provided that after the 24th of August, St. Bartholomew's Day, all clergymen refusing to subscribe to the newly revised Prayer Book, or whose holy orders had not been confirmed by episcopal ordination, would be deprived of their livings. Rather than comply with the "Bartholomew Act," as it came to be known, about 1,200 clergymen relinquished their benefices. Further repressive legislation followed: in 1664 the Conventicle Act forbade, under pain of imprisonment and for a third offence, of transportation, the assembly of five or more persons not of the same family for religious observances where the forms of the Established Church were not used. Next year appeared the Five-Mile Act, which barred nonconformist ministers from teaching school, or from coming within five miles of a corporate town or city, unless they swore to the illegality of bearing arms against the King and pledged themselves not to "endeavor the alteration of government in Church and State."

These measures naturally drove Presbyterianism underground. The ejected clergy usually continued their ministrations in private, and Lowe's diary records many a "private day of prayer," conducted by some ejected clergyman in the home of a staunch nonconformist, and attended by the young apprentice. The diary gives us some idea of the confraternal spirit, intensified by persecution, which existed between the nonconformist ministers and laymen, and hints, to those willing to read between the lines, that then as now the social attraction of group meetings helped to fill the empty pews. With many of the ejected clergy Lowe was personally acquainted, and his diary, bristling with references to these men in the obscure post-ejectment period, should be of interest to the successors of Baines and Calamy. These clergymen, conscious of Lowe's zeal and ability, found in him a willing adjutant, reading the *Practice of Piety* at the bedside of a dying woman, praying with another, repeating a sermon, tolling the church-bell.

Presbyterianism was the strongest force in his life. His reading, according to the diary, was confined to devotional works, such as Ambrose's *Media* and Foxe's *Book of Martyrs*. His ventures in verse—for he was an amateur poet, and occasionally inserts an opus into his diary—are frequently concerned with religion and morality. To him God was a very near and real Being, and his own unworthiness a very disconcerting problem: the same man who spends one night over a jelly-bowl of wine in the alehouse may spend the next kneeling in solitary prayer by a ditch on Ashton Heath, oppressed with his "unsettledness" and a sense that God was "highly offended" with him. The man who can write so racily about his adventures with a ram can also periodically express his feelings, whether downcast or fearful or jubilant, in passages of a semi-Biblical style, introspective enough in character, but so stereotyped as to minimize their value to any psychologist who might try to reconstruct Lowe's mind. But hackneyed as these entries are, they ring with an unmistakable earnestness.

The seriousness with which Lowe took his religion involved him in many a verbal fray with the adherents of Canterbury and Rome. Yet he did not permit his religious ardour to turn him into a fanatic; hot as the disputation waxed the contestants usually departed friends, and even when theological rancour sent them off in anger, a reconciliation was generally effected in short order. As

INTRODUCTION

Lowe has it: "each of us ware of differant judgments and each would vindicate his one way, and many times fall into an exceedinge passion, tho it never occasiond us to love the lesse, which I often marked as a providence of God." Staunch Presbyterian as he was, the charge of bigotry cannot be hurled at him. He counted conforming clergymen among his acquaintances—he was married by Joseph Ward, the Rector of Warrington. He made several expeditions to Wigan to hear Dr. George Hall, the Rector there, and Bishop of Chester. He often dates his diary by saints' days.

There is another characteristic of Roger Lowe's which does not fit in with the traditional portrait of the seventeenth-century Puritan. This is his love for music. The effectiveness with which church-organs had been suppressed during the Interregnum is forcibly brought to our attention by the entry: "When we came to Winwicke I went . . . to heare Organes. I never heard any before." Lowe apparently lost no opportunity to hear them thereafter. On a visit to Manchester he went to church, heard the choristers, and was "exceedinglie taken with the mellodie." Likewise at Chester he heard the "organs and quiristers." "Right glad am I," wrote a music-lover in 1662, "that when Musick was lately shut out of our Churches, on what default of hers I dare not to enquire, it hath since been harboured and welcomed in the Halls . . . of the primest persons of this Nation. . . . Thanks be to God I have lived to see Musick come into request . . . and begin to flourish in our Churches and elsewhere." To this Roger Lowe would have said amen.

But it is time to let Roger speak for himself. Outside of the pages of this diary, and an official document or two, there is nothing to be learned about him: time has erased or hidden what records of his birth, parentage, and upbringing ever existed. That he was dead before April 22, 1679 is proved by "a true and perfect inventory of all the goods, cattels, chattels, debts and rights of Roger Lowe, late of Ashton, late deceased," which bears that date.* He died intestate and the administration of his estate was granted to his widow, Emma Lowe—the "Emm" of the diary. He evidently remained a trader all his days: the largest single item in the inventory is labelled "goods beinge in the shop," and amounts to £29 3s. of the £60 6s. 4d. total appraised value of the estate. The Act Book of Chester describes him as a "husbandman," but this means a man of lower rank than a yeoman, not an agriculturist.

Appended to the manuscript diary is an obituary list, entitled "An Account of the Seaverall Names and Persons that are dead in Ashton and buryed at Winwicke," extending from 1671 to 1678, a list of burials between 1661 and 1669, and, on the last page, a list of the kings of the Saxon Heptarchy. But these passages tell us nothing of Lowe, except than he maintained his residence in Ashton, and we have not included them here.

"No editor can be trusted not to spoil a diary," says Lord Ponsonby. I have tried not to spoil this one. It is presented in its entirety—poetry, receipts for diseased livers, and all. The irregular and inconsistent spelling has been preserved in the hope that a certain archaic charm and indescribable bygone atmosphere might not be dulled. The student of the Lancashire dialect, at least, should be grateful for this. I have, however, taken the liberty to provide capitals uniformly where usage requires them, to introduce punctuation, and to apostrophize when necessary, even to the point of adding an occasional "'s". This has been done with the object of rendering Lowe's style more readily comprehensible to the reader. Lastly, I have employed the New Style of dating throughout the diary.

* See Appendix A.

THE DIARY OF ROGER LOWE

JENUERY, 1663

1.—Friday. Ann Barrow sent for me this morneinge. I went and stayd all day. I was some thinge sickly, yet all day I was feareing the exceptance of love, and att last she vouchsafed a time for consideracion. This evening when I came home I answerd an envitation and went to Thomas Heyes', and should have beene there all night, but would not; came home att 1 or 2 aclocke in night.

2.—Saturday. I was sent for to Robert Rosbothom and was all night and

3 day, Lord's day, we came to chappell; Mr. Madocke[1] preached. I was ingaged in the Ale house att a weddinge of Isibell Hasleden, and promisd to go into Reinford[2] with them.

4.—Lord's day. I was envited to go with Thomas Tickle and his wife into Reinford. John Hasleden went with me. We rid of Raphe's 2 mares. The reason of our goeing was to avince[3] to old Sephon the young couple's mariage. We came thither and the old man seemd to be displeased, but it was but a while. The next day

5, Tusday, we went to Chappell to Lawrance Gaskell's,[4] and spent each man 4d., but old man payd all. Thence we went to Barington's and did likewise. It began to be late and I desird to go home, and moved John Hasleden to go. Old man plaid upon me, which made me willinge to go, but John would not go, being invited by his unkle to stay. I parted; came home my selfe in darke night—a very sad night—and as I came in Ashton near Widow Marshe's old James Hanys lived[?] over against, and was nearly drowned.

6.—Wedensday. My brother cald one me to go with hime to take a house and ground near Pisley windy mill, but we tooke none. We mett my Cozen Hugh Low; went to Ale house. I spent 6d. and soe parted.

7.—Thursday. I went this night to Thomas Heyes on purpose to read over some writeinge for hime.

11.—Lord's day. John Bradshawe came from Leigh to see me. I was very sad all day, but the Lord is my comfort.

14.—John Battersbie, sometime Leigh's schoole master, came to towne, and I was with hime all night and

19 Jenuery.—Tusday. I went into Goleborne[5] to James . . . mith for to gett in some monys. From thence I went to Ann Barrowe's, and I suposd she hid her selfe. Att last I parted from house and she came after me, but I returned home with discomfort, tho I was very much satisfied; for I went with a purpose to free my selfe and not to have nothinge to doe with her.

26.—Tusday. John Parr of Tilsley Bangs[6] beyond Leigh came to town and forced me with hime to go to Alehouse, which I did, and it cost me nothinge. I was att this time very sad in spirit.

FEBRUERY, 1663

3.—Wedensday. I was all day indeavoringe to rectifie some things between old John Jenkins and his sonne Mathew, who ware att suite, the one against the other;

and after a peace was concluded and all things rectifide in and amongst them, we all went to Alehouse togather, and I made Bond for to pay such a summe of moneys att such a time, and so parted.

Thursday. Roger Naylor and Richard Twisse came, and would have me to goe with them to Alehouse. I went, and very mery we ware. I must not spend a 1d., but yet I did.

5th. Friday. I was much troubled att a buisnes that befell about writeing a letter for Ellin Ashton to her sonne Charles. She related that I writt to have her sonne come downe, that she knew not of—which was a false lye.

6.—Saturday. This morneinge I went to Ellin Ashton's and spent 2d., and peace was concluded, which was matter of great satisfaction to my mind.

8th.—Munday. I went to Thomas Holly's and William Chadocke's to buy swines grasse,[7] which I did, and when I came home I was very pensive and sad in consideracion of my povertie, and I sunge the 24th psalme, and after I was very hearty. God will comfort and suply the wants of his poor servents, and God att present deny [w]orldly things, yet if in the meane while God put com[fort?] into hurt, this is better, and that God that gives . . . [illegible].

MARCH, 1663

1.—Lord's day. Att night I, being somewhat sad, resorted to Ashton Towne Heath, and there pourd out a prayer to God, being aside of a ditch. Att my returne I found Thomas Smith, and he would have me to goe to Mr. Woods',[8] which we did, but I stayd not. Mr. Woods lent me a booke.

7th.—Saturday. I was sent for to Christopher Bate to Brinn,⁹ and I went, and very Joyfully. To my joy I was payd the debt oweing to me per Mr. Brinkes, and very Joyfully I came home.

11.—Wedensday. My Master came to Ashton and I was halfe afraid of his anger, but the Lord turned it to best, for he said great deale to me which did very much rejoice me. The Lord's name be magnifide.

15.—Lord's day. Att after evening prayer there was a few went to Mr. Woods' to spend the remaineing part of day. I repeated sermon and stayd prayer, and then came our way.

17.—Tusday. I went to the funerall of a child cald Margrett Hill, child of Mathew Raphe's wife. When we came to Winwicke I went with John Haselden, James Jenkins, Ann Hasleden, Margret Tankerfeild, Ann Taylor, to Mr. Barker's to heare Organes. I never heard any before, and we ware very mery. I spent 6d., and soe we came home.

22.—Lord's day night. I went to Mr. Woods', stayd prayer, and Edmund Winstanley would have me home with hime to supper, and I went with hime.

24th.—Tusday. Went to Leigh.

29.—Lord's day. Went with John Hasleden to Wiggan,¹⁰ and when I came home I was scarcely well. We stayd drinkeing att Georg Burdekin's house.

APRILL, 1663

Lord's day. I was in a troubled condition in my mind considering my unsettlednes, and that God was highly offended with me. Therfor I went into Ashton Heathes and kneeld me downe in a ditch side and made my prayer to the Lord.

6.—Munday. Old Mr. Woods went to Chewbent,[11] and I brought hime one his way.

9.—Thursday. Mr. Woods returnd againe and cald on me, told where he had beene and how he had made peace betweene Mrs. Duckewild of Bickerstaffe and her son James. He seemd to be very glad. I went to bring hime towards home, and he told me he light of a receite for diseases since he went, and puld out a paper and lent me to write out. Told hime he had made it him selfe, as I supose he did. This it was:

An healinge receit for a diseased liver.

First fast and pray, and then take a quart of repentance of Ninivah, and [pu]t nine handfulls of faith in the bloud of Christ with as much hope and charitee as you can gett, and put it into a vessell of a clean conscience. Then boile it on the fire of love so longe till you se by the eyes of faith a blacke scumm of the love of this world . . . [illegible]. Then scum it of cleane with the spoone of faithfull prayers. When this is done, put in the pouder of patiance; then straine altogather in the cupp of a humble hart; then drinke it burneing hott next thy heart, and cover thee warme with as many clothes of amendment of life as God shall enable thee to beare, that thou maist sweat out all the poyson of wantones, pride, whoredome, idolotrie, usury, sweareing, lyeing, with such like, and when thou feelest thy selfe altred from the afore namd vices, take the pouder of say well and put it upon thy tongue; but drinke it with thrice as much of do well daily. Then take the oyle of good workes and anoint therwith eyes, eares, heart, hands, that thou be readie and nimble to minister to the poor distressed members of Christ. When this is done, then in God's name arise from sin willingly, read in the Bible dayly, take up the crosse of Christ boldly and stand to it manfully, bear all visitations patiently, pray continually, rest thankfully, and thou shalt live everlastingly and come to the hill of joy quickly, to which place hasten us, good Lord, speedily.

12.—Lord's day. Being comanded by my Master to come to Leigh I went, and measure was taken on me for a suit of clothes. Att noone my Master and I went to see his child, which was nursd at Morles. From thence we went to John Hindley upon Mosse side,[12] for he was sicke, but our cheife occasion was to se John Chadocke, who lyed sicke att Mr. Whithead's in Astley. We stayd awhile; then we came home, and I came to Ashton.

13.—Munday. I went to Warrington to buy comodities.

15.—Wednesday night. I went to Mr. Woods' to be all night. Mr. Woods had a private day of prayer. He would have had me to have come, but I said I durst not.

23.—Thursday. Mr. Woods came to take leave of every inhabitant,[13] and cald upon me. I went with hime, and with great lamentation at his going, with advise to every family to live welle.

24.—Friday. John Woods came to shop and gave me these verses followeing, being made by a minister in prison, a Nonconformist:

Though I am shutt from Thy house and my one,
I both enjoy in Thee, my God alone.
First for Thy servent I to prison went,
Now for Thy Son to prison I am sent.
For biden prairs was my treason then;
For that was Daniell cast int' lyons' denne.
The wheele is turnd: preaching is now my crime;

Was it not so in the Apostles' time?
Rejoice, my soule, and be exceeding glad!
Such measure in old time the prophets had.
Paull in his hired house in bonds did preach;
In neither I permitted am to teach.
Father, blesst b' Thy name, Thy kingdom come,
Thy will be done though I remaine dumbe.
My bonds e'en preach now, e'en Thy Word be bound,
Prelate e'en once more falls to the grounde
And never rise againe for Thou hast putte
All Thy Sonne's enemies under Thy foote.
My Sovereigne one His throne I joy to see,
Thy Sonne sacred is by Thy decree;
My prayer Thou hast heard through Christ and I
Beleeve Thou canst not this request deny:
A wife and children Thou hast given me;
This wife and children I have left to Thee,
Children borne to Thee, and therfor Thine:
Thou, Lord, wilt be their God, for Thou art mine.

26.—Lord's day. I went to Mr. Woods' house with Thomas Smith; stayd prayer. It was the last Lord's day night that Mr. Woods stayed in Ashton, he intending to goe to Cheshire to live. He preacht amongst us out of the 14th psalme, 5 verse: "The Lord is my refuge;" very much effected he was with parteing with Ashton. Gave him 12d., bended,[14] but he would take no leave of me, for he thought to see me often. 1663.

30.—Thursday. I went to Leigh. To my great greefe my Master tooke on me 3 li. that I had gotten with writeinge and had given me where I had lived, as in Warrington, Lirple.[15] I was sent for to Whiteleige Greene this night to one William Marsh, who lay sicke and had seaverall times sent for me to write his will, which I did. John Hasleden went with me in night and William Knowle was there, and I composd the man's will somwhat handsomely.

MAY, 1663

3.—Lord's day. Att noone Thomas Smith and severall young women we assembled togather in feilds, and I repeated sermon. I was this day somewhat pensive this day by reason of some greevences that ware upon my spirit.

5.—Tusday. Being envited to goe to Banfor longe[16] to Ann Greinsworth, I was goeing, and was in Roger Naylor's, and word was sent me my Master was pasd to shopp, soe I went after and overtooke hime, but he was not offended. Afterwards I went to Banforlonge. Att my comeing home I cald att Roger Naylor's and partly ingagd to come beare them company that night; I comeing downe to shop and stayd awhile, and then went againe and privatly ingagd to Mary to sit up awhile to let us discourse, which she promisd, and the maine question was because we lived seaverally that we wuld not act soe publickely as others, that we might live privately and love firmely, that we might be faithfull to each other in our love till the end: all which was firmely agreed upon. This was the first night that ever I stayd up a wooing ere in my life.

12.—Tusday. My Master brought me a suite of clothes, which did much comfort me.

14.—Thursday. I was envited to goe to the funerall of Edward Calland to Winwicke, which I did.

17.—I was to goe to Wiggin with Thomas Smith; Ales Lealand had promisd me she would then and there answer my desire either pro or con in a final ingagement to Thomas. Att this time Mary Naylor and I were solemnly agreed to be faithfull to each other.

20.—Wednesday. John Chadocke came to Ashton to help cast up shop, and it answered my expectation. I desire to blesse God for it, for the Lord hath beene pleasd to blesse it hitherto in my hands.

30.—Sabath day. I went to Wiggan and should have mett John Chadocke, but he came not.

JUNE, 1663

3.—Wedensday. I was envited to goe to Mr. Leanders' house and I went. Att my comeing home I mett with Mr. Leanders, and he would have me to Ale house.

4.—Thursday. I went to the funeralle of old Mrs. Duckenfeild, first to Bickershawe, then to Wiggan. I thought I should have mett with Mr. Hayhurst[17] and Mr. Downes, but they were not there. I came considering how one day houses, lands, goods, yea and friends and all will leave us, as I particularisd it to her that was dead.

5.—Friday. I was adopted to be sonne and twindle[18] with Richard Bordman of Ashton, wherein we had a great . . . [illegible].

6.—Saturday. I made 3 bonds for old Jenkins.

8.—Munday. I went to Roger Naylor and Mary cryd to me, said she would have nothinge to doe with me, was highly displeased att me; but in the conclusion she was well pleased, would have me goe with her day after to Banfor longe, and she would goe before; and to signifie she was before, she would in such a place lay a bough in the way, which accordingly she did, and I found it upon

9, Tusday, upon my goeing to Banfor longe and att house I found her. As we came home we went into a narrow lane and spoke our minds walkeing to and fro, and ingagd to be faithfull till death. As we ware comeing I saw John Chadocke goeing home, haveing beene att Ashton bringeinge me a parcell of cloth. I cald one hime and get hime backe againe.

15.—Munday. A tedious stitch tooke in my backe, so that I was unable to stay shop, and held me very sore till noone, and then the Lord helped me.

16.—Tusday. I was sent for to Runners feld to be all night, but I went not.

17.—I was Invited to goe with Sarah Jenkins to John Naylor's, of Edg Greene.

21.—Lord's day. I went to Leigh, and there Mr. James Woods came into church, was lately maried Thursday before and his wife was now with hime; and att noone I went into George Norris's, where he was, and sent for hime into a chamber where I was, and when he came he sent for his wife, that I should see her. Att night I came to Sushey, and there I mett with Margret Wright, Mr. Sorowcold's maid. She needs would have me with her home. I went and she made much of me. I came from thence to Roger Naylor's and there they ware att super. I went with Mary and other wenches to a well bottome of Towne Feild.

22.—Munday. I heareing that old Mr. Woods was att John Robbinson's, I hasted to goe see hime, which I did. There we sate and discoursed awhile of the times, and they tooke theire leaves of house, and I went with them, they intending to call att Neaw Hall,[19] and there I left them, being greeved in spirit.

THE DIARY OF ROGER LOWE

24.—Wedensday. I went into Windle to my brother's, and he was gone to Warington. I went and fished a litle time, but catchinge nothing I came home.

28.—Sabath day. There was no service att Ashton and I went to Banfor longe and stayd awhile and came home againe. I promisd to go unto Ellin Scott Sabath day after . . . [illegible].

JULY, 1663

5.—Lord's day. After many envitations to goe with Ellen Scott to Holland, this day I answerd her envitation and went to Banfor longe where she lived, and get her readie. So we went to Holland togather, and when we came there it was befor service time. We went into Hugh Worthington's and spent 8d.; so went into church. A younge lad preached. Att noone we went to her mother's in Dorton,[20] stayd diner. Then Elizabeth Scott livd att Ashurst Hall,[21] and she tooke us downe thither as we ware goeinge. We looked up and downe, stood upon a hill and saw the land round about. It's the pleasentst place that ere I saw, a most gallant prospect. Came to Ashurst Hall and Elizabeth tooke us into the chambers, up and downe—a most pleasant place and gallant walkes. We envited Elizabeth, fellow servent, to goe take part of ½ a dozen, which was done. We went togather to one Ascroft's, and as we went we gat winbery.[22] From thence we parted and came home.

8.—Wedensday. I was in a sad condition of mind, for Roger Naylor was from home and Mary would not assent to have me come thither, but I went and she was somethinge displeased. She went give Calfe drinke; I followed her and there we speake to either, which was very satisfactory to both, and the other day after she came to shopp, and was very glad to see me. Said shee,

"Am not I a wise wench to ingage myselfe thus?" Att those times my effections ran out violently after her, so as that I was never contented one day to an end unles I had seene her, and cheefely my effections were sett upon her virtues and womenly quallities.

13.—Munday. I went to Leigh for comodities, and my Dame was brought to bed. She sent for me into parler for to get her some wine from Ashton. I said I would come againe and bring her some, tooke my leave, and came home. I was sent for to Bainfor longe to Anne Greinsworth to write letters to London and Preston, tooke my leave, and came to Roger Naylor's house, the Cabinet that received the choice of my effection. Her father was not att home. She gave me an handkercheife because I was hott, to dry me with. I went and bought wine and set forward to Leigh; when came thither I went to see my sister, and Robt. Reynolds went and gave me ½ a dozen, lent me his watch. The other day I came home, and when comen I went to Roger Naylor's, and there Mary was put in fright with her father concerning me, for which shee reserved the telling of it till another time, but it was matter of much trouble to me. I was sent for to Banfor longe and I went, but it was with a sad heart, for I sincerely loved her—and now what a greefe is it that such amicable freind as love is, such a freind as is desird every where and without which a comon weale, nay, a family wuld not subsist, yet that this freind that we two have made choice of above all other, yet that there should be such acters and abetters against it as her father and others! Some cry "Murther O!", others cry "Let hime remaine silent in the cabinet of our hearts," and indeed that's our resolution till mallice and spite have said theire worst and best, and then weele advance this our freind to the highest protection: till then we will be silent.

15.—Wedensday. I sent Tho. Smith underhand to

Mary to know all the buisnes, so the buisnes was litle; she was put in affright and sent for me to come the other day.

16.—Thursday. I went and we went into parlor and very sorowfully we ware att some buisnes. We concluded to be more privat and keape more faithfulle.

16.—Thursday. Att night James Naylor came and asked me to goe with him to Neawton, which I did. He wood Anne Barrow, and she sent for us to Stirrop's, where we came and get into chamber where she was, and after a while parted.

18.—Saturday. I set forward to go to Thelwalle in Cheshire to old Mr. Woods, for I had promisd hime to come, and as I was goeing in Warington I went into Mr. Pickering's shop and stayd awhile, for it rained. I bought a booke of Mr. Love's, being his last sermon.[23]. I sat forward, and upon Latchford Heath there ware a great compeny of persons, with 2 drums amongst them. The young men were playing att prison barrs,[24] where I stayd awhile to see them, but concluded it was but vanitie. Came to Mr. Woods', where they ware glad to see me.

19th.—Lord's day. We went altogather to Limme[25] church and

20th, Munday, I came home.

22.—Wedensday. Richard Naylor came over and sent for me, so I went, and we went to Leeche's. I spent 6d. Att night James Naylor asked me to goe with him to Neawton, as formerly, so I went, and we ware sent for to goe to Mr. Collier's, so we went and stayd awhile. Anon Mr. Collier comes in drunke and falls in discoarse with James, and James being not able to defend hime selfe, I tooke hold and answerd to the well likeinge of James.

25.—I rid upon one of Raph Hasleden's horses to Leigh to our child's christeninge. He was named Edward.

AUGUST, 1663

1.—Saturday. I went to Winwicke to the funeralle of old John Tankerfeild. I hasted home and went to see Mary Naylor, for she was scarce well, being troubled with tooth ach.

2.—Lord's day. Mr. Wood sent for me into Hadocke[26] to Nicholas Burscoe's, where Thomas Smith and I went and stayd pra[yer] and so came home.

7.—Friday. Old Mr. Woods came to towne to me, and Peter Lealand, William Knowles, William Hasleden, Thomas . . . [illegible] ware altogather in Alehouse, very merry.

9.—Lord's day. Mathew Lythgo, Edward Bradshaw, Robert Reynolds came frome Leigh, sent for me to Tankerfeild's and had wenches that mett them. We ware all afternoone in Ale house. The Lord forgive us.

12.—Wedensday night we were alltogather in Thomas Leeche's, takeing leave with Thomas Greene haveinge his apprentishipe ended.

18.—Wedensday. Richard Naylor came over out of Yorkshire and Henry Low and I ware with hime very mery, and ware adopted brathren.

19.—Wedensday. I was sent for to Banforlonge to cast up Anne's accounts.

21.—Thursday. I was in Ale house with Roger Naylor

when we parted. I was som what effected and betooke my selfe soliterily into Townes Feild, and there kneeld me downe on side of a came butt[27] and prayd.

23.—Lord's day. Att night Tho: Smith and I went to Robert Rowbotham's to be all night; the other day

24.—Robert gat us plumes. We hasted away, for there was a race to be runne from Goleborne Stockes to Ashton towne. I gat a horse and ran with theme.

28.—Friday. I went to Wiggan; there was a pedler lived there, one Humphrey Starbotham, who ought me some monys, but I gat nonne.

29.—Thomas Smith and I went to Edward Clarke's to be all night. As soone as we ware gotten into house he told us that Ales Lealand was lately dead that eveninge, a very godly younge women.

30.—Lord's day. Mary Naylor frowned one me all day and I was very much troubled to know the reason and cause of it, so I went to bringe Anne Greinsworth towards home, and att my returne homeward I went into house and found her alone and wild her to tell me the reason of her frowneinge, but she would not; but I was very much troubled att it. But I comitt all to God, for my trust is hime. I had before this time presented my service to Ellin Marsh of Ashton, who had a house and liveinge, and kept a private mediator to intercede for me, from whom and by whome I received answer that she would give me the meeteinge ere longe, onely I must be sacret, to which I promisd I would. The Lord worke for me which way may be most for His glory and my comfort and direct me what best to take in hand and order all my effaires.

SEPTEMBER, 1663

1.—Munday. Roger Naylor was gone to Chester, and I went downe and Mary and I went into parlour and talked 2 howres att least, and she cryd to me and seemed to be very sad, and the reason was because of fear of her freinds, lest they would never respect her; so she would have us part. I was endifferant, tho sadly troubled, but ere we parted she was very mery because she had eased her spirit to me. So we parted, but it was with a further resolution of faithfull and constant effection.

2d.—Tusday. Ellin Ashton came to me to write a letter for her, which I did. Att this present I was very much discomposed in spirit, being troubled in mind in consideracion of my poorenes in the world; but my trust is in God, for the earth is His and the fullnes thereof.

4.—Thursday. It was a rany day and I went with William Sixsmith and John Potter to Whitleig Greene. My intentions ware to see some that owed me monys, to get it and come home againe, but we went into Watt's and spent each man 2d. and made a sett of Bowleinge, for each man 2d. in Ale. I was one to bowle and lost, came home, shutt up windowes and went againe and found them in house, get my mony that I had lost and came home. But a sad eveing and a sad day of sicknes I had afterwards.

6.—Lord's day. My Master came to towne and was something displeasd I came not to Leigh of a Lord's day; but he was not over much angry, but very well pleasd with me. He went to Dock Lane to diner. Att night I, being very sad in spirit, went to Towne Feild and up and down. Att last I get to Towne Heath, and upon a ditch side I read a psalme and sunge part of another and came home being very well satisfied, for the Lord will be a rocke to those that trust in Hime.

10.—Thursday. I was sent for to Banferlonge to Anne Greinsworth to write, and it was a very Rany day. This day Hamblett Ashton was att Warrington buryd, being Munday before hangd att Chester for murder.[28] The Lord preserve us from such practices and such end. Amen.

13.—Lord's day. I went to Leigh and att noone John Bradshaw and I went into Vicars Feild and talked of former things. I was att this time very sad in spirit by reason of my selfe and seeing my father's and mother's grave[29] and pondering of other deaths, for I went round about church to looke att graves of such as I knew.

15.—Tusday. Mr. Woods came to shop to see me, and he told me of his sadnes for Eles Lealand's death, and he deliverd to me a paper of verses that he had made and gave me them to write out, and willd me to come this eveninge to Bates' in Haddocke; he would be there this night, and I promisd I would come to hime as soone as I had writt them.

Some verses I composed upon the sad and serious thoughts of Elice Lealand's death:

Anne Epiteph upon the death
of Elice Lealand, maid of Ashton,
who dyed 29th of August 1663
and was buryd 30 August att Ashton chappelle,
being Lord's day in the evening, and these
verses ware made by Mr. James Woods,
Senior, and was given me to write out
by hime 15 September 1663.

Dear Alice, though thy portion was but small
In riches, beauty, things terrestriall,
Yet of the in ward beauty thou hadst share,

Thy soule adornments ware both great and rare.
What others had in out ward garbe and blee[30]
In in ward graces was made up to thee.
O blessed saint, though thou wast poor and meane,
Thy life was gracious, conversation cleane.
Thou much of heaven hadst, of earth but litle;
Thou hadst the sollid, wantedst but the britle.
Of out ward wealth and riches thou hadst none,
Like Christ nor house nor harbor of thy one;
Thou scarcely hadst an hole to hide thy head,
Yet wantest not a pallace, being dead.
Dead, did I say? that word doth much apalle;
My troubled spirits makes my hart to quaile.
Me thinkes thou art not dead, but still I see
Thy lovely visage present to myne eye;
Thy chearfull countenance I still behold,
Which seemes to me of more than mortell mold.
Me thinkes thy lovely lockes and virgin face,
Thy blessed soule so armd with truth and grace,
So fixed in my thoughts do still remaine
Theile never out till I thee see againe.
Me thinkes I still thy gracious words do hear,
Humble confessions mixt with godly fear,
Thy gracious speech without all taunts or Nipps
Did shew that grace was powred into thy lips.
Thy tongue did still on sacred subjects Runne,
With them thou ended and with them begunne.
Thou hadst a rare and blessed memorie,
Of sacred things a well stord treasurie;
Thy gifts ware not discernd nor seene of many
And yet, I fear, scarce pareleld by any.
Clear, rare perfections hardly could be seene;
Thine inward worth and vertues lay within.
God's holy Word to thee was very sweet,
When naked Word and naked heart did meete.
The wants of nature grace did much suply,
And all its errors sweetly certifie.
Grace made thy life and conversation sweete,

Grace made thee chast, pure, humble and discreet;
The worth and worke of grace apeard in thee
And shined forth in great Excelencie.
Thy heart was humble, thine effections pure,
Thy conscience tender, judgment firme and sure;
Thy smallest slipps did seeme more great to thee
Then unto others sins of highst degree,
And thou an idle word deplored more
Then others some of lyes and oathes a score.
Yea, I have seene thy blubberd eyes to swell
And teares drop downe as from a fountaine well
When with temptations thou hast beene oprest,
Or sight of sine hath brought thee much unrest.
But O! how full of joy and sweet content
Have I thee seene with mirth and merriment
When faith and hope have gott the victorie
And thou hast overcome triumphantly.
Of all condicions thou experiance had,
And knewest how to joy and to be sadd;
Yea, thou with God most sweetly did converse
That it my selfe surpasseth to expresse.
How much of heaven did in thee apear
Whilst thou wast here on earth who will declare?
'Twas but awhile that thou didst sojourne here,
But 'twas with reverence and godly feare;
But thou in that same while more worke didst doe
Then some that twise thy age had lived unto.
Thou madest hast unto thy journey's end,
Longing to meete that loved spouse and freind;
And now thy wearie pilgrimage is past
And to thy heaven thou art come att last,
And thou art hapie and shall ever be
Perfect and blest to all eternitie.
When I the Lives of Popes and Cardinalls
And prelats proud in their pontificalls
Do seriously consider and observe
How men of learneing, parts, and gifts do swarve,
How many that of precious soules have charge

Are careles, covetous, and live att large—
Then thee, poor Eles, I often thinke upon:
That more of God and true religion
Was in the heart of such poor silly babyes
Then in the heart of heads of such learnd Rabies,
Their formall service and outside devotion,
With litle of devine and heavenly motion,
Was far inferior to thy sacred straine,
When with thy prayers teares did flow amaine
And holy, fervent, set thy heart on fire,
That it did kindle such a stronge desire
That thou didst seldom from God's presance parte
Till God had heard thy prayers, cheard thy heart.
Thou seldom partedst from God's presance sad,
His soule refreshments made thy heart most glad;
With hidden manna thou didst often meete,
And God's returns unto thy soule was sweete.
And though thou nothinge hadst yet thou hadst all,
For thou hadst Christ who was thy all in all;
Thou hadst content in that thy poor estate
And so wast richer than a potentate.
Christ was thy portion, Christ thy food and clothinge,
Christ was thy treasure . . . nothing.
Thou dyedst rich though scarce a penny had,
Thou now art joyful, though here often sad;
And yet more sad for others then thy selfe,
Thou nere wast sad for want of wordly pelfe.
In greatest wants thou allwayes had anough,
Thy way was pleasant, wheither smooth or Rough.
Thou fedst on promises in time of want
And livedst in Christ when other things ware scant.
Thou thy poore calling chearfully didst follow
When pyneing cares did others seeme to swallow.
Thou now triumphest in those joyes above,
Sorrounded all about with peace and love.
Thy warfare now is finisht, race is runne,
Thou est kept the faith, th' jubilee begunn;
All teares from thy eyes are wipet away,

Sorow nor sadnes make no longer stay.
Thou now art perfect and for ever blest
Where we thee leave to thy eternall rest.
Sorie I am I was not att thy death,
When thou expired thy last and sweatest breath,
Nor att thy funerall some teares to sheede,
As parents for their children that are dead.
Yet, to expresse my true respects to thee
These verses here a monument shall be,
Which may perhaps not without teares be read
When I as well as thou am buried;
And I doe hope that longe it will not be
But I, blest saint, shall blessed be with [thee].

     Sic finitur lacrimationes
15 September   amicorum Jacobus Woods.
 1663   Rogerus Lowe.

After I had written this I sett forward according to my promise to follow him, and att Henry Bates' in Hadocke I found hime att prayer, for Henry's sister was distemperd. As soone as he could leave them we walked 2 feild's breadth and parted, both being very sad. I came to old John Rob[inson]; they would have had me to have eaten, but [I] stayd awhile and then parted, onely I let hime se 4 verses I made upon his not remembrance of me in a letter to Ashton, which I had intended to have writt in a letter and sent it to hime.

When I into your letter once did see
And bee-held no remembrance of poor me,
Then to myselfe I said, "Hodge, thou'rt forgot,
For he in his letter Lowe remembers not."

att the readinge of which he laughed heartily.

17.—Thursday. I went to bowleing Alley and lost 12d., att which I was sore greeved, came home, and this evening I went with James Naylor to Neawton awooing Ann Barrowe. She had sent for me to come speake with her. I went to Mr. Collier's to fetch her to us into widow Heapy's, for there we resided. I put of my one hatt and put on another, and made also my[selfe] as if I ware John Naylor's man and was sent to towne upon an occasion, and so had something to speake to Anne from her sister. Get her out, and she, with much requesting, promisd to come to us after supper, which shee did; desird me to meete her att Winwick, Lord's day after.

17.—Friday. I helpt att the desire of old John Jenkins to picke sheaves of Barley of carte.

18th.—I was in a great perplextie by reason of Mary Naylor, who was too strange to me in her effections.

19.—Lord's day. I went to Winwicke with James Naylor to meete Anne Barrowe according to my promise. I went, but she could not come. We came to Heapy's att noone and stayd drinkeing 8d.; then, being sent for by her, we went into Mr. Collier's and [were] taken into parlour, and I conferred with her awhile to move her to exceptance. After awhile I left her and hime to their best discourse.

21.—Munday. John Bradshaw came from Leigh to see me and we went to Gawther's and drunke, and then afterwards went to Brinne to see a Race, but it was runne before we came, so we came to shop againe.

22.—Tusday. Nicholas Corles of Abreham[31] came to towne to me, tooke me to Ale house. I went and brought hime a gate[32] towards home, and so parted. This night Mary Naylor came to me and spake kindley to me, to my great satisfaction. This night John Hasleden was pretty merry, and he goes to John Potter's and sends 6d. for Ale, and sent for me. It was made in a jelly bowle and I was sent for to the drinkeing of.[33] Att this time I was neither mery nor sad, but in an endifferant state, rather in greefe; but the Author of my faith and hope is fixed in God. He can, He will redeeme me out of all my feares and greefes; I shall se better times wherein I shall have further occasion to blesse the Lord.

24.—Thursday. Eles Lealand came from Mr. Woods' in Cheshire. I brought her towards home; we talked of Eles Lealand's death. In the close of her discourse she desird me to do a message for her to Tho. Smith from Mr. Woods, which I promisd I would—and because Thomas seldome came to shop and I could not see hime I writt the Arrend downe to hime and in bottome of pag I made and writt these verses:

> Your freindship's like the morneing's deaw,
> No sooner comne, but bids adiew;
> With other objects you are taken
> And litle Hodge is quite forsaken.
> But I'me content: let it be soe,
> Though freinds will nere freinds them put fro.

This afternoone I went downe to Roger Naylor's, and Mary and I talked togather. After she and I ware parted James and I went to Leashe,[34] and when I came home there was a direct N and halfe of M providentially made upon my breeches, plaine to view in any man's sight, made of mire with leapeing. I looked upon it to be from providence, and fortold somethinge in my aprehension. The smallest of God's providences should not be past by without observetion.

25.—Friday. I went to Roger Naylor and Roger was gone to Wiggan to a buryinge and poor Mary was sicke in bed. I went to her and hild[35] and stayd awhile. She promisd to send Joseph to tell me how she did. I parted, and when I came to shop Raph Stirrope, my father,[36] send for me to Gawther's. I went.

26.—Peter Lealand came and I writt Mr. Woods'

verses for hime. This night there was a Robery done att clay pitts; a younge man was stricken of his horse very timely in night and his monys taken of hime.

27.—I went to Leigh and gave me Master 5 li. 10s. Att my comeing home Margret Naylor cald of me and enjoined me to come to their house when John Naylor was away. Att this time I was somewhat greeved in mind by reason I saw not those smileing providences of God, as others have. But it's good to waite on God.

28.—Munday. John Hasleden and I with some others were in Tankerfeild's and ware merry. John and I begann to bett each with other, which was contrarie to custome that we should so act one against another.

29.—James Naylor envited me to their house. I went and found Mary alone and very pleasant. This night I sange in shopp by a candle the cheife verses of the 71 psalme with alacritie and heart chearfullnes.

OCTOBER, 1663

1.—Thursday. I had goods sent me from Leigh in a Cart, being come frome Chester faire, and I was in a very harty condition.

2.—Friday. I went to Roger Naylor and Mary and I sate togather in parlour and discoursed to both our satisfactions. I came to shop and anon John Chadocke came and brought me some comodities, told me that my Master intended to have me home, and that some of his ladds should be set up in Ashton, all which greeved me extramely. But it's best to fly to the helpe that never failes, and to hold one still waiteing one God. He who hath brought me through infancie and youth will not now leave me nor forsake me, for my trust is in Hime.

3.—Saturday. I ecqueinted Mary Naylor with my thoughts about these former things above said, about my departure from Ashton, att which she was greeved and would have me speake to my Master. I was all this day sad, yea, very sad in heart, but there's a God to comfort a discomfortable soule when we see nothing in ourselves but miserie, nor nothing in world but trouble. Then looke up wards, looke up to God; I will looke up unto the Lord. I will waite one the God of my salvation; my God will heare me. I went this eveninge with James Naylor to Neawton to Ann Barrow awooing. She had beene sicke.

4.—Lord's day. My brother came to Ashton. I told hime how that my Master intended to take me home. He was sory in the thinge, but hoped all might be for best.

5.—Munday. Mary Naylor sent for me to their house. We talked togather concerneing our privat matters, and this morneing she promisd never to marry any except my selfe.

6. day—Tusday. I was sent for to Thomas Heyes to Reckon with them, and they owed me 3s. 10d., and I said 2s. 10d., . . . was mistaken.

7.—Wedensday. I sent them word this day. My Master sent litle Thomas to me for me to teach, which greeved me very sore.

8.—Thursday. William Scofeild, a mercer in Warrington, came to Ashton and envited me to goe with hime to Ale house, where I did, and we talked about tradeinge and how to gett wives.

11.—Lord's day. It was a rainy day, and I was very negligent in my duty to God. The Lord forgive me.

12.—Munday. I had a packe of candles came from Leigh. I was somwhat merry at this time in consideracion of Mary Naylor's love to me, the consideracon therof amidst other greefes. Yet that is comfort to me and much rejoices my spirit in sadnes.

13.—Tusday. I sat in shop all day. Onely I went up Greene to old parson Lee's[37] and John Haselden and Thomas Rosbothom and we alltogather jesting. Thomas Rosbothom and John Hasleden attempted with either of them a good kibbow[38] to suprize poor parson and I in parson's shop, but we defended our selves awhile, but in Conclusion I was glad to creepe up into a loft to secure my selfe, but was taken att last and sufferd efliction. I made them to laugh in telling them how once I was hurried with a Tupp[39] in a Rope, who comeing towards Leigh with Tupp in feilde, the tupp sett upon poor Hodge and so geper knowd [?] me that in the conclusion I cryd out. But none heard me, and I, being onecqueinted how to act with tuppe in Rope, let hime have the length of Rope, and tupp rann all wayes backewards and fell one me, so that I was put in a terrible fright what to doe to save me shinnes. I was almost in a . . . [illegible] condition. I layd me down with my head opon my leggs, thinkeing to save my leggs, and he gave me such a patt on the head [as] made me turne up white eyes. I thought and was halfe efraid lest I had gotten old Nicke on the Rope. I prayd to God to deliver me from the tuppe and Rope, but in the conclusion my bones ware sore, braines sicke, and heart dead with feare what to do with tupp. I looked att tupp with an angry countenance, but could not tell how to be revenged. Kill hime I durst not —then I should have had the labour to have caryd himme, which I could not. Faire words would not pacifie hime nor angry countenances efright hime, but att last I resolved upon a manly resolution thus: "What, Hodge? art in a streite? What's the reason of thes feare and greefe? A tupp. A tupp? does that daunt thee?

Stand upon thy leggs and fight manfully in answer ther unto!" I did, and gett a kibbow out of hedge, and tupp and I fell to it, but the tupp orecame me. I could doe no good, but downe on my knees againe. I get hold of tupp's hornes and of one of his feet, and cast hime. "So now, tupp, I intend to be revenged on thee," and smote hime on the head. But with great difficultie I gat hime to Leigh, but I nere was in such a puzle in all my life as I was with that tupp. When I saw the tupp set on me, so I though: "What have I gotten on Rope? A sheep is a harmles creature, they say. What is this, old Nicke?" He did so nicke me up that he made me to leap and friske. I exercisd feet, hands, tongue, and all members of my body was exercised about tupp head. Sometimes shaked in revenge braines troubled how to be revenged, tongue in uttering most wofull lamentations and sometimes loud bankerings [?], but since then I have knowne tupps, the very name of tupps hath been trouble to my eares. I remember another story which once was to my greefe, as well as this which occasions me to remember it, likewise that the world may see what streites I have beene in and what troubles I have undergone in my life. When I lived with Mr. Livesey,[40] he sent me to High Lee[41] to Mr. Henry Lee about a minister for his chappell, and going from Budworth to High Lee without victuals I came just att diner's time. Mr. Lee was att diner. I sent letter to hime; he sent word I should stay diner, which I did, and was very hungery. I was sett att table with servents. Every servent a great bowlefull of podige, anon a great trencher like a pott lid I and all others had, with a great quantity of podige. The dishes els ware but small and few. I put bread into my podige thinking to have a spoone, but none came. While I was thus in expectation of that I could not obtaine, every man haveing a horne spoone in their pocketts, haveing done their pottage, fell to the other dishes. Thought I, these Hungery Amallakites that I am gotten amongst will devour all if I doe not set upon a resolution. I, lookeing towards them to see theire nimblenes in the exercise of their hands from dish to their mouth, made me to forgett my hunger, but I cast my eyes from them, thinkeing it ware best to bethinke my selfe of my one hungery condition. What would it advantage me though I was sat there to table and not satisfie hunger? I cast an eye to my trencher—there was a whole sea of pottage before. Thought I, what must I doe with all these; wished in my hart many times that those hungery Rogues had them in their gutts, but that would not doe, for still they ware there before me, and I durst not set them away, tho it was manners so to have done. Well, I resolved: "Hodge, if thou will have any victualls here, thou sees how the case is and into whose compeny thou art falne into, what a hungery spirit possesses these men. Thou must now resolve upon action;" and a speedy dispatch with these pottage accordingly I did, and sweeped them as if I would have drunke. Than when I had them in my mouth I was in such a hott fitt in my mouth [as] turned meditation into action, but att last, to my lamentation, I was werse then before. I would gladly have given 5s. that I had but had the benefitt of aire or a northern blast. My tongue in my mouth was in a sad condition; helpe my selfe I could not, for table was before me and a wall behind me upon my backe, a women with her flasket[42] upon right hand, and a man with his codd peece upon the other, and in this sad condition I sat blothering,[43] knew not what to doe best. Those few pottage I tasted was both diner and supper. I att last rise from table with a hungery belly but a lamenting heart, and ere since I have beene cautious how to supp pottage, and likewise wary. Nothing werser to a man then over hastiness, especially in hott concernements: hott women, hott pottage, and angry tupps be ware of and pray to be deliverd frome.

13.—Tusday. Att night I went with John Hasleden into Hadocke; he had a letter come from London, and he went to gett a workeman to come and helpe hime. It was a very rainy night and filthy gate[44] and very darke.

15.—Thursday. Att night old Ezibell envited John Hasleden, Dicke Asmull, and I to drinke with her son in law. We went in night, but before we went I was somewhat disconsolate, and was in shop, and Mary Naylor came into shop and we stayd togather, and it did satisfie me very much. She would have me to bringe her over brid[ge], which I did. Afterwards, when I had taken leave of her, I went with some younge folkes to this man's house, and by vertue of Marye's compenie it made me as hearty as might be.

16.—Friday. I was sent for to Thomas Heyes'. I went. When I came thither it was but upon shop effaires. I sett forward to Banfer longe; there I stayd and dranke Botle Ale and Common Ale[45] and was very merry. Set forward for home; when I was about Roger Naylor's I went in, and Mary was angry with me [that] I had beene out of shop, for folkes had beene there enquireing for me, which angred her very sore, soe shee was troubled att me.

17.—Saturday. I had a very sickly day, but the Lord instigated the paine. My love was very earnest to Mary att this time. This night was a sad night to me in paine of my head, but the Lord was favorable to me in the morneing, for I was in health. I blesse God: weepeing may endure for a night, but joy comes in the morneing.

18.—Lord's day. I went downe to Mary when her father was come up to chappell. She was very respectfull to me. I was not harty this day, but in a sad condition.

19.—Munday. Ann Greinsworth came to towne to goe brew att Lodge. I was glad to se her; went and brought her to Ellin Ashton; spent 2d. on her.

21.—Wedensday. I went to Roger Naylor's. As I came againe att Thomas Naylor's I bought a Henn and 6 chickens for 6d. Afterwards Ann Barrow sent for me to John Naylor's. I went and we conferred togather of time and place, when and where James and I must meete her. But in this discourse I intreated for my selfe to be the next in succession if in case they two should breake of, to which she did not say no, neither yea. When I parted I sett forward to Banferlonge, where Ellin Scott did very joyfully entertaine me. After I had gotten refreshments I came home.

22.—Thursday. Roger Naylor and Thomas Insworth came up towne to me and envited me to Ale house, and Roger said it should cost me nothinge, soe I went, and when we ware togather we ware discourseing of Esop's fable. I was spakeing of the fable of dogge and peece of flesh, who, swiminge over River, caught shadow and lost substance. Says Roger, "Take [care] of you doeing so," which speech did much amaze me, for I was troubled att it very sore. But I made my prayer to the Lord and the Lord releived. He is my shepheard; He will provide. Therfore I fear not. This night James Low and I went togather to Banferlonge and stayd there till far in night. There was Ann Marsh there, who hee wood, and Ellin Scott and I talked of other things. I had a great cold that troubled me very sore.

23.—Friday. Roger Naylor went from home, and I went to house and Mary and I sat togather in parlor, and it satisfied me very much.

25.—Lord's day. Ann Barrow came to Ashton and gave me a letter to answer for her into Yorkeshire to Richard Naylor. This eveninge old Izibell and John Hasleden and I went to Gawther's and ware merry when we parted. We went all togather into old John Jenkins'; we thought he would have dyed this night. When I was with hime he shooke me by the hand, and I conferred with hime. After awhile I parted.

27.—My Master came to towne and was very loveing to me, wished me to gett all the monys I could against Christmas. Henry Low came to town and would have me to speake to Elizebeth Hindley for hime, which I promisd to doe this evening. I went with James Naylor into Goleborne awooing to Ann Barrowe. I was att this time very sad in spirit, for I had not seene Mary of a good while.

28.—Wedensday. Mary Naylor went to Warington and stayd all night att her unkle John Lowe's in Hoome,[46] and upon the

29.—Thursday, I went as far as to Neawton[47] to meet her, but I could not light of her and came home again in a sadd Fitt. This night John Hasleden and I went to Banforlonge and ware very wellcomly entertained, and as we came home we talked of wenches. He told me that he loved a wench in Ireland, and so the day after I writ a love letter for hime into Ireland. Att this time I did love Mary extreamely, and was sad I could not see her nowithstanding.

30.—Friday. She came to me and was very loveinge which did very much satisfie me.

31.—My Brother's wife came and brought me nutts and victualinge. This night I went up Greene to Mary, but could not have the oportunitie to speake to her.

NOVEMBER, 1663

1.—Lord's day. Mr. Woods came to towne. He was att William Hasleden's att diner. I went to bring hime a pipe of tobacco, but could not stay, for I was ingagd into Compenie. Ann Barrow and James Naylor and we ware alltogather at noone in Gawther's. Mr. Woods left word with Izibell that he would goe to Robt. Rosbotham to be all night, and he would have me to come to hime, so att night Thomas Smith and I went thither, but we went away by Peter Lealand's. Thomas sent me into house and he stayd of me. When I came to door they were singing psalmes. I went in and Peter would have me pray, but I was unfitt att that time and so desird excuse. Wenches and we went altogather to Robt. Rosbotham. Thomas Smith and I ware altogather, and he spoke low and told us he intended a Comunion Thursday night next att James Lowe's, Neawton Commin.

2.—Munday. I went downe to Roger Naylor's and Mary was not so favorable to me as I conceived she should be, and I was troubled very sore.

3.—Tusday. It was Ashton Court,[48] and I was to sue John Robbinson; he had given his word for Robbin Taylor. It was a great trouble to my spirit. My Brother came to me this night and was all night with me. I was up till far in night to hear vardict.

5.—Thursday. Att night I went to James Lowe's of Neawton Comin. There Mr. Woods was and a compeny of Christians, where we receivd comunion and Mr. Woods preacht out of 7 Ecclesiastes, 14 verse. Mr. Gregg[49] was at prayer when I came in. It was a joyfull night and a sad night.

7.—Saturday. Att night I went with Thomas Rosbotham, James Lee, James Naylor a foomert hunteinge,[50] but we catched a hedge hogge, but nothing els.

8.—Lord's day. Att night Richard Weinwright came to me and said he would go to Bainforlonge. I said I would goe with hime if he would let me ride behind hime, which he promisd to do. Anon Ellin Scott came rideing from Holland, and her mother was on foote waiteing att Roger Naylor's. When we mett theme I would have turnd home againe, but they would not lett me, but sett me behind old women on horsbacke, so we ridd like Irish folkes. When we came there we spent night in feasting and discourseing, and att 10 of the clocke in night Dick and I tooke horse and parted.

9.—Munday night. I went with James Naylor to old Barrowe's in Goleborne to woo Ann. It was very darke and stormy and late in night ere we came home.

12.—Grace Garard had an Ale, cald neighbors, went to spend monye. I went with them and spent . . . d., and I came home to bed and left neighbors and musicke and all.

13.—Friday. Jane Wright, Mr. Sorrowcold's maid, came to towne and we ware very merry togather. I accomodated her with Ale, and so we parted. I was att this time in a very fair way for pleaseing my carnell selfe, for I knew my selfe exceptable with Emm Potter, notwithstanding my love was entire to Mary Naylor in respect of my vow to her, and I was in hopes that her father countenanced me in the thinge.

15.—Lord's day. It was a very rainy day day [sic] and Mr. Blakeburne[51] came not to chappell, but sent Mr. Barker[52] to read, and I was som what troubled. Old Roger Naylor came and sate with me all afternoone. This day was not well spent, I must confesse. The Lord humble me for it.

16.—I kept shop all day and had a fire. Old Roger Naylor came to me and Thomas Smith, and we spent each of us 1d. for Ale. I was very heartles att this presant.

18.—Wedensday. I was sent for to Banforlonge and cald att Thomas Heyes' and received 8s. for comodities. Then went to Bainforlonge, where I was accomodated with Ale, and when I had writt some accounts for Anne I parted and came to Roger Naylor's, where Mary was busy. I had a deale to say to Mary, but could not have the opertunitie, soe came to shop.

20.—Friday. I was sent for to Bainforlonge to Ann Greinsworth to write a letter to London to her Brother, and I went.

22.—Lord's day. I went to Leigh and cald of Ann Barrow, and shee tooke me into parlour and gave me spiced beere and we conferred awhile. I spoke much for my selfe by way of motive that shee would except of me, and after awhile parted, being enjoined by her to come att noone backe againe. I went to Leigh and att noone John and I went to Twisse barne to see all those preparatives in readines to the casting of Leigh great Bell and third bell, both which Bells lay in steeple.[53] We came up to Richard Darwell and spent 2d. and came into towne and so parted. I sat forward for home and by the way cald on Ann Barrow accordinge to promise, but she was sent for to goe into Pemberton; but she left word I must stay till shee came, but I would not. But Elizebeth Hart told me that shee said that if shee thought her father would dye soone she would waite for me, because I had presented my effections to her, and this shee said upon better motive to her for me. But yet, the greefe of all was behind, for Bett told me how perfidiously and knavishly James Naylor had dealt with me, for he wooing Ann would allwayes have me with hime, and I had some effections to his sister, and had sent her seaverall litle notes, which shee putt in her box, and this one eveninge, the 9th of this presant November, and he cald for a band and Mary bid hime go take one out of her box, so he rifled her box up and tooke all my letters, which I had

THE DIARY OF ROGER LOWE 47

sent her att seaverall occasions, and tooke them in his pockett, and when we came into Goleborne to Barowe's I went into parlor to John Hart and he followed Ann into another chamber and let her see my sacrets to Mary, and I had writt in one that I wishd Mary would be as faithfull to me as Ann was to hime, and this stinkeing Raskell betrayed his one sister and me, who I went allwayes with and spent my monys for his sake and advised hime the best I could. Nay, and above all he backebitt me, and said it would doe well if I could gett monys against my comeing out, and said I durst never come in his father's sight, which was a lye. He said as soone as his sister angerd hime he would tell his father of all—and this is the acteing of a seemeing pretended freind to me as can be, when in truth is no better then a deivelish, malicious, dissembleing, knavish rascall. Butt Ann was displeasd att me att first, tho caryd nobly and loveingly to my face, but Bett Hart told me this that I might know my freinds from my foes. And now it's best to gett and feare God for a freind, for we see man will faile us and world will faile but God will not faile those that trust in hime. But this was matter of much greife to me and I was very sad upon it. I tooke leave from Bett and cald att old James Damme's. John, his sonne, did manifest abundance of love to me, gave me aples, brought me to Edge Greene, made me to promise to come att Christmas. So that the Lord will not leave me freindles in this world.

23.—Tusday. I went to Roger Naylor's. He was gone to Chester and I told Mary all above writt and of all James' knaverie to me and to her, and she was highly offended and was very respectfull to me. Att night she sent for me; James would have me be all night with hime, and she told me what she had said. I did not stay all night, but came to shop to injoy bed, and as I was comeing I mett with Richard Worrell of Warington, apothecarie, and John Earle, who tooke me with them to Ale house.

25.—Thursday. I kept shopp all day, onely Ann Barrow and her sister came to go to Peter Kenion's, and I brought Ann towards that place and spoke my mind to her concerneing James' fact[54] against me. I was very much displeased concerneing it. When I came to shop I was very sadd all day after, but God is my comfort and tho I walk in greefes, yea, in the vale of death, yet then God's rod and staffe will be matter of comfort to me.

1 DECEMBER, 1663

Tusday. Being Warington faire I kept shop all day, being very sollemne and sad. Henry Low came and we discoursed togather about all our effaires and greefes. I went with hime to bottome of Towne Feild and there parted with a joint resolution that what we said each to other should lye dead. This night Richard Naylor came to me, wished me to come down to his father's house, which I did. He was very sad concerninge Elizebeth Seddon's acteings to hime; wishd me to compose a letter to her in his name, which I did.

6.—Lord's day. I went to Leigh. John Chadocke's wife was brought to Bed att noone. I parted with Leigh and came towards home, and cald att Henry Barrow's in Goleborne, but Ann Barrow was gone frome home, so I came forward to Roger Naylor and stayd supper— Roger forced me to stay. I was very glad to see that respect I see I had from them.

9.—Wedensday. I went to Beinforlonge, was very much made of, tooke leave and came to Thomas Heyes' and stayd awhile, and then came home.

11.—Fridey. Att night Henry Low came to me for to goe with hime a wooinge to Thomas Heyes' to Anne

Hasleden. She tented[55] her sister, who was lyeinge in, and Ann had moved me sundry times to gett Henry [to] come, and this night we both went, and had spiced drinke, and very much made of we ware; but it was a very darke night and we stood without a great while . . .

[Two pages are gone from the diary.]

[JANUARY, 1664]

17.—Saturday. Being envited and leave granted by my Master to goe to Hughe's Hindley of West Leigh, this day I went with John Hasleden and ware all night, and other day we went to Leigh and then backe againe to Hughe's; after dinner went forward for Ashton.

FEBRUERY, 1664

1.—Sabath day. Att night I went to Mr. Woods', and we being some younge people that som times associeted togather, and providence seemeing to make a breach amongst us, we ware sore discomforted, some in theire removall far of and I my selfe in thoughts of beeing removed out of towne.

2.—Munday. We went againe, viz., Thomas Smith and I, being envited, intending to have spent the night to the edification of one another. Att this time I was sore discouraged in regard John Chadocke, my fellow aprentice, was in goeing from my Master, and knew not how God would dispose of me; but the Lord is my trust, and in God is my confidence.

5.—Thursday. Before day my fellow prentice, John Chadocke, cald me up with Will Parkinson, John Hindley, and others. He was going to be maried, and had stolne his love away from Mr. Whitehead's, and my Master gave assent I should goe with them. I gate a horse of William Sixsmith and we went altogather to Billinge Chappell[56] and stayd att Humphrey Cowley's till 2 came againe from fetching Mr. Bispam. When they came they brought word we must meet hime att Holland att one Thomas Prescott's. We tooke horse, came thuther, get the ceremonie overpast, and dined. I was sent afore to Wiggan to buy 7 yards ribbin, and they came into Wiggan. We each of us had a yard of ribbin of 12d. per yard, and so rid through towne. I saw them through towne and so parted. I was all this while in a sad hart.

13.—Friday. Thomas Smith came to me to goe be all night att Mr. Woods'. I went and Mr. Woods and I sat till far of night talkeing about ministers and other things. He said Mr. Callamy,[57] who was put in prison for preachinge one Sabeth day, had above 500 li. given hime in one weeke's imprisonment of his beloved people.

15.—Lord's day. I went to Leigh, and as soone as I came there my Master and Dame both said I must have measure taken of me for a suite of clothes and a coate, and Taylor came att night to take measure of me. But my Master would let me have nothinge but a coate, soe I would have none and parted with greefe, and as I came I overtooke Hugh Hindley and I told hime my greefe. He bid me feare not; he would goe to hime the other day and would move hime, but the consideracion of this moved me to great lamentation. In my comeinge home att noone Robert Reynolds tooke me into George Norris's, and we 2 with Clarke ware mery awhile and then parted. Afterwards we went into Robt Feilding's and ware with Thomas Naylor, and he would let me pay nothinge, soe we parted and went to church.

17th.—Tusday. I went to Leigh very early, and soe early as I tooke John Chadocke in bed. He opend shop door and he went to bed againe. I sat att bed's feete and we talked of every thinge, somethinge about his marige, and about what had hapend upon Lord's day about clothes for me. And att this time I expected some anger from my Master, but he said nothinge to me; but John told me my Dame was displeasd that I should be so hasty. Nevertheles amidst all . . . my trust is in the Lord.

18. Febwedensday. Widow Low came and gave me 1s. for a sermon writeinge.

22th.—Tho. Smith and I went to Mr. Woods' and ware all night. Mr. Woods was gone to the funeralle of his wive's mother, soe I repeated sermon. There was foure younge folkes presant stayd on purpose to hear repetition.

28.—Saturday. Tho. Smith and I went to Robert Rosbothom in Parke Lane, being very welcomly entertained. Our discourse was about these times; and the other morneing, being Lord's day, I was excercisd to pray, and after we had had prayer with a chapter and psalme with other things, we came towards Ashton chappell, being envited to come againe. But this time I was very sad in consideracion . . . providence towards me . . . The greater will in time not deny the lesse, and why should I fear? God's providence is the poor man's inheritance, and God hath anough in store for me, for the earth is the Lord's with the fullnes therof. Therfore it's good to waite and trust in the Lord.

10.—Wedensday. I went to Thomas Heyes' and Beinforlonge to reckon, and att this time Ann Greinsworth was perswaded I loved Ellin Scott, and I satisfied her to the contrarie. I writt her some letters and so parted.

14.—Att after eveninge prayer I went into Ale house

with one Roger Lowe and spent 4d., but had a very sickly night and

15.—Munday, I had a very sad, sickly day all day, but the Lord strengthened me.

19.—Friday. I cast up debt bookes and see how I stood with my Master, and my charge was to my Master that I had in goods from my Master 148 li. 8s. 9d. in one year, and his receit in mony from me, and in debts, 135 li. 5s. 1d., and in that year I cleared the shop to my Master within 13 li. 7s. 7d., and this did rejoice my spirit.

21.—Lord's day. I went to Leigh and stayd till noone, and Mr. James Woods was there and envited me to his house all night. I went to hime to Georg Norris's house att after dinner and spent 3d., so parted. Thence I went to see my sister Katherin, gave her 4d.; so came to my Master and parted, and intended to Hugh Hindley's, for John Hasleden was there and I was to come to hime, but I mett Hugh and family towards church, and John was gone for Ashton; so I parted and came my selfe and cald on my sister Ellin and so parted, and as I was comeinge near Barrowe's Ann Barrow cald of me, for we had beene out one against the other; so I went to her. Shee tooke me in to parlor and we rectifide all buisnesses, so I came away.

25.—Thursday. Thomas Atherton was to part with neighborhood, so I was envited amongst neighbors to go to Ale house to drinke, and John Potter and I begann to discourse concerneing the manner of God's worship. He was for Episcopecie and I for Presbittery. The contention had like to have beene hott, but the Lord prevented. It was 2 or 3 dayes ere we speake, and I was efraid lest he should doe me some hurt, and I went into house and all anger was removed.

MARCH, 1664

6 day—Lord's day. I was very pensive and sad all day, and I betooke my selfe to solitarines, for I walked downe to Town Heath and presented my suplication to the Lord. I prayd to God and showd hime all my trouble and I hope the Lord heard, for I was abundantly comforted in my spirit.

8th.—Tusday. John Hasleden, James Jenkins, and I walked into feilds. John Hasleden had ingagd himselfe to Dicke Asmull night befor, in a drunken humor, to serve hime as aprentice for 4 yeares, and we contrivd how to gett hime of in the feilds. This night I was in a troubled condition, for Sarah Hasleden spoke in a backebiting way of me, and she would tell her brother of me, but all was in a causeles matter, for me spendinge 2d. But she was handsomely taken up in my behalfe by John Potter of Lilly Lane and by her husband, and God onely is my defence.

10.—Thursday. Humphrey Harrison came to shop and stayd with me a great while and att last moved me to instruct his son in teachinge hime to endite letters and to cast account up, which I promisd I would doe. This night I was envited to goe to Gawther Taylor's to drinke Braggod, for wife bought her comodities of me, and she said if I would not come, then farewell; so I was constrained to goe, but I stayd but for a short time.

11.—Fridey. Ann Barrow came to towne and moved me to write a letter for her in answer to a love letter from Richard Naylor. I did, and movd her to sett her one name. Mr. Maddocke and old Roger Naylor ware in shop and ware very earnest to see letter, but I would not let them. Mr. Madocke and Roger wishd me to goe to Ale house with them, which I did, and after Mr.

Maddocke went with Roger home to be all night, and they stayd on me till I had shutt up shop, and I went downe to Roger's with them and stayd supper and prayer, and so came to bed.

12.—Saturday. Mr. Maddocke came with Roger Naylor and envited me to Ale house and as we ware drinkeinge James Astley, a Wiggan man, came into house and gave me a letter with a lemmon, which was a token sent from Richard Naylor from Wakefeild in Yorkeshire. This night I had promisd to goe to Robert Rosbothom's house, and did, with Thomas Smith with me, and was all night, and they lent me Mr. Gee's booke concerneinge prayer;[58] he was minister at Eccleston. And upon the

15th day, Tusday, I was readinge in his booke, and in consideracion of the man's person and gravitie I was posesd with sadnes and composd these verses:

Renowned Gee, thou now enjoyest glory,
Yet thy name shall remaine earth's lastinge story.
In thought of thee, ah! I can sitt and weepe
That thou by death shouldst now be laid esleepe.
How lovely was thy life, joyfull thy death; } sic cantat
Angells receivd thy soule att latest breath. } Rogerus Lowe
I'le say no more, but weepe, yet would joy to see
My selfe in hapines with blessed Gee.
Gee now in joy triumphs, his sorrows past,
And he that place enjoyes that aye shall last.
Therfore, blest Gee, this once I'le bid farewell,
Hopeing ere longe t' be there where thou dost dwell.

His name was Edward Gee, minister att Eccleston Church; he dyed about or in the year 1660 or 1659 or therabouts. But the church of God sustained great losse in his death and Mr. Herle's[59] of Winwicke and Mr. Johnson's[60] of Hallsall, who all flourished and dyed about this time aforesaid, in so much as it was the lamentation of Mr. Coleborne, att Leigh excercise in his prayer, that we now wanted our Herles, our Gees, and our Johnsons. This was upon the 25 December, 1660. Old Mr. Woods joined with hime.

17.—Thursday. My sister Ellin came to towne of Ashton to buy comodities of me. Her husband was not well. I brought her to Town Heath. I moved att parteinge to serve God and go to church and labour to instruct her children in the wayes of God, and in so doeinge God would blesse her and make them comfortable to her. I was att this time sad in spirit, but God will refresh.

18.—Friday. I was sent for to John Naylor's wife, of Edge Greene, and I was in some greefe by reason of Cooke's wife, a very wrathfull, malicious women, had reported that I said such things concerneinge women's naturall infirmities, which I never did, and troubled me extramely. But the Lord will prevent all my feares and will procure respect for me.

20th.—Lord's day. Lidia Scott and Joseph Scott and Raph Bradshawe came out of Dalton beyond Holland, and Lidia came to me for to have me to goe to them into Tankerfeild's. I did, and att night I went to bringe them towards home, and soe parted.

21.—Munday morneinge. Sarah Hasleden sent to me to come write a letter for her to London, which I did. This day John Hasleden came into shopp, and James Jenkins, and I said I had a brasse shillinge. "Oh," says John Hasleden, "I have another. Come," says he, "lett's goe to . . . Baty's; we can gett them of." It was concluded one and we all went, and when it came to the effect of the buisnes, John's 12d. she receivd, but mine she would not, and they ware both in the hand of James Jenkins to give her. So John Hasleden bid us goe; he thought he could move her to take it in our absence, but it could not be. James and I waited of John's compenie home, but he came not. We resolved for home, and when we came home we gat our super. John still came not; I was ill troubled that we had left hime. We resolved after super to sett thither and went, and so we mett hime in the way and came togather into towne and went to John Jenkins' and there spent each 2d. and ware merry in consideracion of our actings.

22.—Tusday. I was sadly sicke and had a very sicke night, but the Lord restord me in the other morneinge.

25.—Friday. John Naylor's wife came to town and wishd me to goe with her into an Alehouse. I went.

27.—Lord's day. Ann Greinsworth came to towne and wishd to say nothing, and she would let me se a buisnes, and she pulls out a love letter writt in Roman hand with R L in the conclusory, and this was found before gates att Bainforlong, directed to Ellin Scott. I was something displeased, but the matter was of small vallue. This day John Grimsheye's prentice came and borowed of me 3s. 6d., and so ran away from his Master. He borowed it in his Master's name, and his Master lived in Goleborne.

APRIL, 1664

1.—Friday. I was sorely troubled in my mind, for I had given Roger Naylor, senior, great occasion of offence in telling hime of a letter being found writt in my name, and the occasion being his, as I suposd, and I particulerizd the buisnes as if he should be the man, and he was highly offended att me, which was my great greife. But God will help.

THE DIARY OF ROGER LOWE 57

2.—Saturday. John Hasleden and I went into his Brother's ground to see Colepits, and this afternoone Thomas Smith and I went to Thellwell to Mr. Woods' and stayd till Munday, and as soone as we came thither, after a short rest, we went to Gropenall[61] church to visit one George Clare, who lay sicke, and I went into church yard to looke att graves, as it is my common custome, and there stayd awhile admiringe the common frailtie of mankind: how silently now they were lyeinge in dust. It being somwhat late we parted to Mr. Woods' the next day.

Lord's day. We went to Limme, Thomas and I, and heard one Mr. Grimshey out of the 36 psalme, 8 verse. Att noone we came home and stayd to hear Mr. Swetnam att Thellwelle out 1 James, 12.

4.—Munday. We sett for Ashton and att Latchford Heath we mett with Roger Naylor and Peter Aspinwolle[62] att a litle Alehouse; we went to them. I spent my 2d. with them and soe parted to Warington, where I calld att Mr. Scofeild's shop, and John Naylor and he ware togather. He sent for Ale for me. We discoursed awhile and then parted, went into Stationer's shop and Thomas Peake's shop, and so bid farewell to Towne; came to Ashton, and seaverall had enquired for me.

5.—Tusday. I writt to Richard Naylor in Wakefeild in Yorkeshire.

7.—Friday. My Dame sent me 4 new bands[63] which pleasd me very well. This night old Peter Lealand came to me, and sit in shop a good while, and att night I went to bringe hime towards home, and we talked of times and about Mr. Woods. After a while we parted.

9.—Easter day. I went to Leigh and att noone John Chadocke and I went to Latley Comon[64] to a house cald

Sumnor's to se one Ann Smith who was there in Hold,[65] that had drownd her child in Hurst Ground, and she was very much greeved, as she seemed. She sate att chimney's end, hangeing downe her head, and I spoke to her to move her to repent, told her God was mercifull: he pardond Devid, who was adulterer and murderer. I came away being very sorowfull for her; came to Leigh Church, and he was att his sermon. Mr. Woods' maid would have had me gone home with hime, but I refusd.

11.—Munday. I was pensive and sad and went into Town Feild and prayd to the Lord, and I hope the Lord heard.

12.—Tusday. Thomas Naylor sent for me to make a bond betweene hime and Mr. Byrome. I did. He gave me 6d. and the neighborhood of Ashton envited me to goe with them to Ale house this eveninge, which I did, and spent 6d.

13.—Wedensday. Ellin Scott came to towne, and Roger Naylor did woo her, and there was some difference betweene hime and me, and now he sent for me, and this eveninge all was in love and I was glad. We see God can make them who somtimes [are] enemies turne to be freinds.

15.—Friday. I was envited to goe with Ann Taylor and Elizebeth Taylor to William Anderton's in Pemberton, and there was with us John Hasleden, Emm Potter, and others. We stayd till after sunne goeinge downe and then parted; came to Goose Greene and there stayd in an Alehouse, but it was my great trouble to stay or to have gone this gate, onely they ware good customers to me and I durst not but goe for fear of displeasure.

17.—Lord's day. I began to write sermon this morneinge. John Potter and wife and John Hasleden invented to efright me in tellinge me I was cited to Bishop's Court for Nonconffornitie to Common Prayer; so att noone John Hasleden and I came together to diner and he seluted me with this: that I was cited, at the heareing of which I eate no more, but went to Town Heath and prayd to God to deliver me and consulted with my selfe how to doe. But att noone it was found out, and I was glad.

18.—Munday. I writt a letter by the advice of Peter Asmulle to John Hasleden from his unkle from Reinford for John Speedie comeing to Reinford, and I sent letter down towne by a stranger; and upon the other day, being Tusday, John hasted for Reinford—away he hasted this day. Lee Bowden, Steward att Lodge, and Roger Naylor and I ware togather in John Jenkins' and old Mr. Woods came to shoppe and thought much I was in Ale, warned me to take heed. I told hime I could not trade if att some times I did not spend 2d.

20.—Wedensday. John Jenkins, Constable, tooke John Hasleden and my selfe to every Ale house with hime in night, in answer to a warrant to make pri[vate] search.[66]

24.—Lord's day. I went to Leigh and I cald on my sister Ellin; they gave me a Cocke chicken. When I came to Leigh young Mr. Woods' wife did very earnestly envite me home with her att noone. John Chadocke and I went into feilds, and in a feild cald Horse Shoo we sat us downe by a great pitt side and conversed togather of our greefes concerneing our callinge, and att night he brought me to West Leigh Heath and our discourse was the same.

27.—Wedensday. Younge John Jenkinson and I went to looke Bird nests out in feilds and my legs ware cruelly pricked. I was att this time in great fear because shopp was to be cast up and I was efraid it would not answer my Master's expectation. Now the Lord helpe me through my prentishipp, that I may be freed frome these sad charges of goods I stand indebted with, and am so posessed with such feares by reason of my ingagements to my Master I know not how to rest. The Lord keape me from miscaryinge, for the Lord's sake!

MAY, 1664

1.—Lord's day. I was som what pensive all day in consideracion of my unsetlements in this world, but yet much comforted in trustinge in God. Their not so hapy as have these worldly enjoyments as those who have God for their Lord. Ann Greinsworth very earnestly envited me to Bainforlonge, and I promisd to comme.

3.—Tusday. Henry Feildinge, an Hower glasse maker whom I had hower glasses of, came, and I was ingagd for 1 dozen and $\frac{1}{2}$ of hower glasses, and this day I payd hime and made meet with hime and upon

4th May, being Wedensday, I tooke 30 glasses more, and he intended for Leigh and I writt a letter to John Chadocke to move hime to take some of hime, and a very honest man he was to me. I had them of the rate of 10s. a dozen and sold them after 12, and he gave me $4\frac{1}{2}$ hower glasses and 6d. in monys when I payd hime.

6.—Friday. John Chadocke came from Leigh to cast up shop, and efraid I was least I should not answer my Master's expectation. Att after we had cast up shop we went to Heath a shooteinge, came to towne againe, and supt att younge John Jenkns', and was there all night. I slept litle, expectinge to go to Leigh the other morneinge, which I did betimes in the morneinge, John and I togather. When we came to Leigh I was ingaged to my Master 200 li. and up wards, and it pleased God to

THE DIARY OF ROGER LOWE 61

blesse my indeavors that I had profited my Master 21 li. 1s. 5d. I was glad; then I boldly speake my greevences, and my Master told me he had bought me a steake and would give me ... of it. I had measure taken of me for a new dublett, and was to have a new hatt and a new pair stockins, and my Master told me he intended shop for me and att Michealmas next I was to go with hime to Chester faire. And thus the Lord favord me and turnd my feares into joyes. Praise the Lord, O my soule!

8th.—Lord's day. This eveninge Richard Bordman was very ill. I made his will this night.

9th.—Munday. I went with Richard Weinwright to Nicholas Bursco's marle pitt; gave marlers ¼ tobacco.

10th.—Tusday. I went to Bainforlonge to Anne Greinsworthe, but stayd not.

11.—Wedensday. I went downe to Roger Naylor's. He was from home and I spoke Roughly to Mary and shee seemed to be very effectionate, but I litle matered it. I cald her a false dissembleinge harted person. She tooke it heinously.

12.—Thursday. Lawrance Pendlebery was maried this day, and he intreated my compenie. I desired excuse, but this eveninge I went and spent 6d. with them, and parted.

14th.—Saturday. I went to my Brother's into Windle and upon the

15th day, being Lord's day, Tho. Smith came to me and we went 2 and 2 togather to Cowley Hill to hear Mr. Gregg preach att one Mrs. Harper's, in the parlor. There he preached out 3 Mallichi, 15, 16, 17, 18 verses.

When sermon was done we came to my brother's. I was not well, but departed from my brother's sicke; but the Lord suported me, that ere I got home I was pretty welle.

17.—Tusday. Ann Greinsworth sent for me to Bainforlonge. I writt a letter for her to her Brother, then in London. She made much of me. I sat downe all her accounts att this time. I came away by Roger Naylor's and spoke my mind to Mary Naylor, which was not excepted, though was very favorable to mee; and I set her light as she did to me, and so I parted.

19.—Thursday. I went to Billinge Chappell to a race and James Darbishire sawe me and envited me to goe with hime into Humphrey Cowley's to spend 2d., he beinge come from Bolton. So I went, and in the spence of 2d., Nicholas Houghton came to us [as] we ware in Butterie, and he begann to give disdaininge words out against the Art of a grocer or mercer, and so particulerized it as to me in so much as I was very angry, in so much as Humphrey Cowly's wife was angry att me in a very furious manner, and I was sadly troubled. Yet the wife went out, and some compeny as she went out too comended me highly, in so much as she came againe and made a recantation for what she had said, and I was better satisfied.

20.—Friday. John Jenkinson and Joshua Naylor and I went togather to take a throstell[67] nest, and by chance we mett with a py annot[68] nest. We tooke [it]; every one had one pye, and one we gave to Tho. Winstanly, and so came homme. Old Jenkins this day came and payed me for making his will and other things. He payd me 11s. 9d., tooke me to Ale house and spent his 6d. on me. This night John Jenkins, Constable, and I went togather to lay night hookes, but

21.—Goeing, there was nothing found.

THE DIARY OF ROGER LOWE 63

22.—Lord's day. I went [to] Wiggan and heard Mr. John Blakeburne preach. I dinde att Eles Leigh's. John Jenkins and wife ware both with me.

24.—Tusday. John Naylor's wife sent for me to write a letter for her to one Mrs. Shaw in Nesson[69] in Worrell in Cheshire, and I went and she made much of me.

28.—This morneing I went betime to Leigh, and was pretty hearty in my returne.

30th.—Munday. I went into Billinge and bought tenn dozen of syth stones for to send to Leigh. I was in a pensive condition att this time.

JUNE, 1664

4.—Saturday. Gilbert Naylor came to me to have me to goe with hime to his sister Margrett's into Houghton. I went with hime this eveninge, and att Castle Hill[70] in Hindley he would have me to goe into Astley's, an Ale house, and as we ware drinkinge Robert Reynolds, junior, of Leigh, but now of Blackerhead,[71] came in. He was just now sett up att Blackerhead. He was glad to se me. We stayd drinkeinge of 8d. and I payd not a 1d.; so we parted and came to Houghton Common and went into William Rycrof's house, and William discoursed and told us many things concerneinge Dean Church, Mr. Tilsley,[72] and Mr. Eanger,[73] who being a conforming manne and now beeinge att Deane Church began to quarrelle. We parted from thence and went to Hugh Rigbie's—that was the place we intended too—and they ware in bed. Wife gets up, makes a fire, gets us supper, and we go to bed with an intention to go to Deane Church in the morneinge, but we lay too longe in our beds. After dinner we sett towards home. When I came to Ashton Mary Naylor had a sweet heart comne, and I was som whatt greeved and went to Towne Heath and meditated upon these words: "It's good to hope and quietly to waite." Observation: that hopeing and waiting for a possible thing is a Christian's duty in time of difficultie.

13.—Munday. Thomas Jameson was in Jenkins' and sent for me to come drinke with hime, and we stayd late in night, and we began a Controversie. He, a papist, beganne to speake revileingly of Luther and Calvin, which I labored to defend, conceiveinge them to be meere Callumnies of the papists because of his revolt from his friership. We ware in love and peace in our discourse.

14.—Tusday. Att night Raph Hasleden sent for me. His youngest daughter was dead; it was conceived she had eaten Asnicke,[74] for Sarah had laid Asnicke in meale and in Butter, and the child getting to it gett that which was laid in Butter, and so dyd; and he intreated me to go to Warington to Mr. Finche's to gett them [to] come to funerall, which I did, and cald at Winwicke and bespoke bread and drinke, and when I came to the formost, Mrs. Finch would not let me goe till the next morneinge, for it was late. So I stayd and att day I arose and went to sadle horse, and so came homme.

15.—Wedensday. My Dame came to the funeralle, and sent for me to come and bring all monys with me I had, to pay funeralle expences with. When we came to Winwicke they causd me to set down in seller to take account of flaggons drawen. I rid home, and att Thomas Rothwell's we stayd drinkeinge, but the

16th day, Thursday, I lay all day sicke, but was much comforted by Emm Potter's care of me.

20.—Munday. I went to Beinfor longe and was much

made of, ecqueinteing Anne Greinsworth of a servent maid she might have.

21.—Tusday. Mathew Low and I ware falne out a litle and he came to shop and we went to Ale house and ware reconcild.

23.—Wedensday. I went to Leigh and gave my Dame 9 li. in monys. She would have the Taylor take measure on me for a paire of Breeches, dublett, and coate, and she and I went into shop to looke out cloth, and she made me take my choice, soe we tooke two Remlents[75] into house and she kept them in her custodie. This newes sent me joyfullie towards Ashton. It was the Lord that movd her; nay, she was so forward as she would have had the tailor left others' worke for to have done my clothes against Sabbath day.

26.—Lord's day. Edmund Winstanly envited me to dinner with hime and I went.

JULY, 1664

3.—Lord's day. I went to Leigh. I had a new suit of clothes and a coat. I went to William Gerrard's and we discoursed awhile concerneinge my time and other things; so I parted. Att night my Dame would not let me goe till I had supd. I came to Ashton and went to John Jenkins' and anon Mr. James Sorrowcold came into house, and he spent 6d. on me. I brought hime home, for he tooke me alonge with hime, and I was all night, and I lay in his chamber.

4.—Munday. Betime in the morninge I came home, and John Chaddocke was come from Leigh and had some odd comodities of me. I brought hime a gate towards home.

5.—Tusday. Very early I went to Leigh.

10.—Lord's day. I was envited per Widow Taylor to ride before her daughter to the funeralle of Thomas Taylor of Sankey Halle, and I assented. Raph Hasleden and his wife and Elizebeth Taylor rid altogather. This eveninge I was all night att Sankey Hall; there was att Hall a younge man, a papist named Robert Kenion. He and I conversed longe togather about papistrie, and after our discourse he was very loveinge.

11th.—Munday. Early I got up and went to Warington, and in Mr. Pickering's shop I found parator[76] Dicke Tildsley, and Ale he would give me; so I went with hime and stayd awhile, and so parted. Came to Mr. Worrelle and payd 3s. 6d. and so went to Hall; there was wine and bisketts to be had. So about 11 clocke he was fatched out and led on a coach to Winwicke, and this is the conclusion of this story, by which we may se how that one day freinds and world and all here below we must part with: the grave is the parting place. Freinds that did much honor this funeralle came to attend it to the grave, and there parted. Now the Lord grant us such grace as, tho we may part with freinds and world, yet we may never part with Christ, and that will be our comfort.

14.—Thursday. I was with Daniell Chaddocke and Dr. Naylor in the Ale house, and I was very sicke.

15.—Friday. I went to Warrington to buy candles of Richard Nichols. I had but 4 dozen, and I brought them home upon horseback.

17.—Lord's day. I went with Thomas Smith to St. Ellin Chappell,[77] and we cald on my brother and refreshed ourselves with victualls, and so went to chappelle.

It was a very rainy day. Mr. Ambrose[78] preached. We came home att noone, and Mr. Asmulle preached at Ashton.

22.—Friday. I went with John Jenkinson to Wiggan and I gatt in that old debt that was oweinge me per Humphrey Starbothome, a pedler in Wiggan.

24.—Lord's day. I went with Tho. Smith to Wiggan, and we heard Bishop[79] preach. Dined att Eles Leigh's. Robert Reynolds was in towne; he gave 2d. in Ale to me, and enjoined me to make for hime an Indenture, because that Wiginers did threaten hime. I parted frome hime, and att after eveninge prayer Thomas and I came to Peter Lealand's and was all night. The other day, comeing home, I mett with Thomas Heyes, who said he had beene att shop att one, but found me not; so he desird me to go backe with hime to William Chadocke's to make up some accounts. So I did and they gave me 6d., so I parted.

28.—Thursday. I was intreated per Richard Asmulle to go with hime and John Hasleden into Hindley. There was a wench had laid a child on hime. So we went, and in Mr. Lanckton's feilds she was, and she ardently manifested hime to be the father of the child in her wombe; so we parted. Att Platt Bridge he tooke us into Hugh Platt's and spent 6d. on us. As I came home I cald att Bainforlonge and Ann was glad to see me.

29.—Saturday. One Mr. Lowe,[80] vicar of Highton, came to towne and would have me to come to hime, and abundance of effection he pretended to me; but att last we began in disputeinge about episcopecie and presbittery. He said they ware apostollicalle. "Yea," quoth I, "they are apostaticalle from the truthes of God;" and he seemd to be displeasd.

AUGUST, 1664

8.—Munday. Being Ashton wakes,[81] att this time I had a most ardent effection to Emm Potter, and she was in compeny att Tankerfeild's with Henry Kenion, and it greeved me very much. Henry Low came to me and would have me to go to Tankerfeild's [to] spend 2d., so we went to the next chamber to that they ware in. Att last they came by us and I movd Emm to stay to drinke with me, which she did, but would not stay with me, neither there nor no where els; would not come to me, tho she said she would; and I was in a very sad eflicted estate, and all by reason of her.

10.—Wedensday. Emme went to bringe one Pegg Lightfoote tords homme and I went after her and we spoke to each other, and Ellin Harrison came unto us and tooke[82] us and was in a great rage against Emme, and this was matter of great greife of harte unto me. But my trust is in God, who will helpe in trouble. Tho the storme be now, yet I have hopes I shall see a calme. This is my hopes and till then I'll waite one God.

14.—Lord's day. I went ot Neawtowne and heard Mr. Blakeburne, and he enjoind old William Hasleden and I to come to Rothwell's, which we did and had 2 pints of wine, which he would have payd for, but I would not suffer it. After I came home I went to Elizebeth Rosbothome, and I spoke my mind to her concerneinge Emme, which I could not doe without teares, and she did pitie my state. I was very discomforted.

15.—Munday. The sun began to shine, for Elizebeth Rosbothom had told Ellin my greefe, and she pitied my condition so as she resolved she would never act against me so. I went to John Rosbothome's and stayd awhile, and both Ellin and Emme came downe, and Ellin went her way and Emme and I went into chamber and there we professed each other's loves to each other; so I was abundantly satisfied within my selfe and I promisd this night to come see her in her chamber. God will arise and show pitie to his distressed servent.

16.—Old Mr. Woods came to towne and was all night att William Hasleden's, and they would have had me to super, but Mr. Woods ingagd me to come to be with hime. I was this afternoone with William Chadocke and Thomas Heyes casting up their accounts, and after I had done with them I came to shop and shutt it up and went to William Hasleden's. They ware att prayer. After prayer Mr. Woods' discourse was concerneinge wars and troubles that he and old William had beene in togather, so att far in night I came my way and came to the window that Emm Potter lay in chamber, and I would gladly have come in, but she durst not let me in; but she rise up to the windowe and we kisd, and so I went to bed.

17.—Att night I went to Docke Lane to get Raph Hasleden to go for me to Leigh to fetch goods. He was not att homme, but I spoke to Sarah and bought 2 li. of waxe.

18th.—Thursday. This morneinge we went with cart, and waters ware up att Penington bridge. We gat our comodities into carte and so parted Leigh and came well homme.

19.—Friday. I borowed a horse and went to Humphrey Burscoe's in Lowton for to buy hony and wax of his sisters, but they ware too hard for me.

20.—Saturday. Constables of Hadocke and Goleborne came to have me write theire presentments for assizes, and when I had donne I writt: "Poore is provided, highwayes repaired, these querys answerd, and clarke unrewarded," att which they laughed most heartily.

22.—Munday. I was desired by Gawther Taylor's wife to ride before Eles, her daughter, to the funeralle of Lucie Taylor of Sankey Halle, and I left my Master's occasions att Ashton to answer their expectation. Went to Sankey Hall, came againe with buryinge to Winwicke, and whiles drinkeinge was I gat Emme into a place above, where we talked about some things, and in this while Eles Taylor, like an unworthy women, went and tooke another to ride before her, so that when I came to take horse there was none for me. I was highly perplexd, yet bore it very patiently. John Moody and I came home togather, and as we ware comeinge John Potter and Emm behind hime overtooke us, and he askd me what I would give hime att Neawton. I promisd hime a quart of Ale and at Neawton he light and we stayd and ware very mery. Anonne Dicke Naylor comes and falls a quarrellinge with me, in so much as we fell to it, but John Potter vindicated my cause nobly and poor Emme stickd close to mee; so they gatt Dicke away with a deale of shame to his part. So we all came togather home, and William Sixsmith would needs have John Moody and I ride behind hime, which we did, and so ridd into towne, but it was night. I tooke John Potter into Alehouse and spent 6d. on hime.

26.—Fridey. I went to Docke Lane to see Raph this morneing, who had receivd a hurt by a fall of a horse as he was goeinge to assizes. I was very much troubled in my thoughts by reason of Dr. Naylor's and mine falling out, but especially my greefe was because of my greatt love to Emme, which by reason of my longe time could not be perfected. But God is alsufficient. Trust in the Lord, O my soule, and thou shalt see the event of all to God's glory and thy comfort in the end.

28.—Lord's day. I went to Leigh. My Master was gone to Assizes att noone. I was very disconsolate, but I went to John Chadocke's house and mett with John Hindley. We went, hee and I, to top of steeple and discoursed of former dayes and passages past and gonne. There was buryd one Sander Sixes, who had his necke broken in rideinge between Dean church and Bent.[83] When we ware come from top of steeple John Chadocke was seekeing us, so we went altogather to Ale house and spent each of us 1d.; so parted. Att night I came home to Ashton and went to see Raph Hasleden, and parted and came to bed.

29.—Munday. Dr. Naylor came to me and we ware in John Jenkins' and made freinds and ware very merry. The Lord worked graciously for me in many respects. Therfore I blesse the Lord.

30.—Tusday. Young Mr. Woods came with his servent to go to Georg Markland's and I gat a horse and went with hime. We dined at Widow Clarke's in Windle. After I came home I went to Robert Rosbothom.

SEPTEMBER, 1664

4.—Lord's day. I was with Mr. Sorowcold's servents in Ale house, and was merry.

5.—Munday. I went to my father Stirrop's to buy hony and wax, and I gat Ann Taylor to goe with me. My father was not att homme, so I bargaind not.

10.—Saturday. I was envited to go to the funeralle of old Asmulle at Sendelly Greene.[84] I went with John Hasleden and John Potter to Winwicke.

11.—Lord's day. I went to Wiggan with John Potter

to hear Bishop, but he was gone. We stayd all afternoone in Eles Leighe's and att night we came home and I went into Thomas Harrison's, and Emm had been with Kenion, she told me, but it was against her will.

12.—Munday. Mr. Gerrard of Bainforlonge came to towne and envited me to Tankerfeild's and gave me the Ale and envited me to his house.

16.—Friday. Att night between the howers of 7 and 8 departed this life Richard Bordman, in Ashton. I waked most of this night. John Potter and I went to Ringe Bell. He dyd of a dropsie.

17.—I went to Winwicke to the interreinge of the same Bordman.

18th.—I went with John Potter to Wiggan to hear Bishope.

19.—Mr. Potter came to towne and I made a Bond for hime and Anne Johnson. He received 20 li. in monys. I made it in hast. Mr. Henry Gerrard came to towne and causd me to goe with hime to Ellin Ashton's. He spent his 6d. on me and envited me to come to Beinforlonge.

21.—Wedensday. Dr. Naylor met me with a younge man with hime, who intreated me to get his sister out for that younge manne, soe I promisd I would do my indeavor. I went to Thomas Naylor and get her leave to go to an Ale that old Harvie's wife had; so as soone as I had her out I conferrd her upon the younge man. So I went away to homme and told Emme what I had done, and she was very angry.

25.—Lord's day. It was a very rainy morneinge, and I was for to go to Leigh, but was prevented by raine. I went to chappell, and att noone, when I came out, it was faire and I sett for ward for Leigh, and I overtooke John Naylor of Edg Green; he would needs have me to goe [to] diner, but as I came againe he light of me,[85] and supd with hime I did; so I came home. I delivered to my Master 12 li. in monys.

25.—Munday. Tho. Naylor and Tho. Greenhough came to me to make a Bond, and they tooke me to Ale house and we ware merry.

29.—Thursday. Gilbert Naylor came to have me make a Bond for hime and William Sixsmithe.

OCTOBER, 1664

2.—Lord's day. I went to the funeralle of old John Jenkins to Winwicke, and att after drinkeinge I went with John Potter and Raph Low, church warden, to Hall Winwicke,[86] and went to see chappell, and went to top of house and up and downe, and then we parted and I came for home, and when we ware come home James Jenkins envited me and John Hasleden to go to his brother's to spend 2d. He had a buisnes to disclose to us and none els. We went, and when we came it was to ecqueint us of his compeny keapeinge with a younge women who was worth 11 li. per Annum in house and ground; and he moved us to go with hime to meet her att Warington the Lord's day after, and we promisd we would.

5.—Wednesday. I went to my Brother's, was all night. His wife was brought to bed, so I was ingaged to go with hime to Prestcott upon Lord's day after. This day the Under Sheriffe of Lancashire, Mr. Robert Greinsworth, came to towne and sent for me. He was freindly with me by reason I write for his mother.

7.—Friday. I went to Wiggan to have a deske made me of James Leythect, but it was not made. He gave Joshua Naylor and me 6d. in Ale, and he would procure a wife for me—Robt. Winstanly's daughter. John Hamson was in towne and spent 4d. on me. Our discourse was concerneing his sonne, to be bound to my Master. When I came to Ashton I heard of a stirke[87] that my Master had sent me, but it was not according to my mind. I was this night with Townmen of Ashton in Ale house.

9.—Lord's day. This morneing I went to my Brother's into Windle. He had a child to be christened att Prestcott, so I was ingagd to be the one godfather and Raph Falster, near Carr Mill, was the other, and my coz, Ann Shey, was god mother. We went to Prescott and drunke att Edward Darbishire's, clarke of church, and Ralph Falster and I went to top of steeple and into church. There was Sextones makeing a grave for one Jacke or Georg Massy, a Runer, who was buryd this day att after eveninge prayer. We went into Darbishire's house againe and stayd and drunke; it cost Raph Falster and me, either of us, 15d.: 2s. 6d. in all, and we payd it jointly. I had intended to have come home, but the latenes of night prevented me, so came to my brother's and stayd all night.

16.—Lord's day. I went to Leigh. Mr. Henmar[88] preached att noone. John Hampson, John Chadocke, and I went to Jane Mull's and had 3 quarts discourseinge about John Hampson's son, who should be my Master's prentice. Att night William Knowles went home with me to Ashton. As I came I overtooke sister Ellin and Mr. Battersbie, whome I wished to speake to my Master concerneinge me. I thought it sad for me to be ingagd 9 yeares to stay in Ashton to sell my Master's ware of and get no knowledge; so he promisd to speake to Hugh

Hindley of it, and they two would goe togather to my
Master and speake my greevences.

31.—Munday. I went to Wiggan and bought 1 dozen
and ½ of twist for coates for Raph Jenkins, and stuffe for
a cap. I ridd. Att this time I was som what troubled in
my thoughts concerneinge my eff'aires in world. This
night I was with John Potter with his freinds that ware
come from Winwicke, in John Jenkins'. I spent 10d.
and att far in night I went to bed.

NOVEMBER, 1664

3.—Wedensday. Ellin Scott came from Beinforlonge,
and Richard Weinwright and I and Peter Buckstone ware
all att Tankerfeild's takeing leave of her. We had a
wessell.[89]

11, 12, 13 dayes.—I was in an eflicted state in my body
by reason of cold, in so much as I could scarcely goe.

14.—Munday. Raph Hasleden sent for me to come to
diner; his child was christened the day before, and I went.

20.—Lord's day. Thomas Smith and I went to Robert
Rosbotham's and stayd till far in night and then came
homme.

27.—Lord's day. Henry Low, Dr. Naylor, James
Naylor, and I had a 12d. sent from Yorke from Henry
Gyles to be drunke amongst us, and this night we ware
togather to spend this 12d. Afterwards I went into
Thomas Harrison's, and Thomas' wife was not welle,
and if I would spend 2d. he would spend 3d., so we sent
for drinke, and I was very earnest to have John Potter
there, and went and fatched hime. So he and John
Hasleden and I, we spent each 11d. apeece.

31.—St. Andrewe's day.[90] I went to Beinforlonge to Anne Greinsworth to cast up her accounts. She made very much of mee, so I came home.

DECEMBER, 1664.

3.—Saterday. My Master sent litle Thomas to me with comodities, and I thought he had over charged them, and it troubled me very much.

8.—Thursday. William Hey came to me to have me go with hime to Wiggan to cast up some accounts between hime and Mr. Totty about the buyinge and sellinge of beasts; so I promisd to go in the eveninge, because I could not deferr my Master's service, but I should do it [at] night. So this afternoone I went to Beinforlonge and cald of hime, and we went togather and ware most part of night, and in the other morneinge came my way; but there was some differances between them, and we did nothinge to purpose.

9.—And when I was come home Friday Mrs. Finch sent for me to Raph Hasleden and intreated me to bringe her home att night, which I promisd to doe.

18.—Lord's day. I went to the funerall of Henry Ashton, son of William de Whitleige Greene. Att comeinge home there was Tho. Harison, John Potter, and some others, and we cald att Heapye's and spent 2d. apeece. So came home, and att John Jenkins' we did as so before we parted, and so bid farewelle to one another when twopeny flaggon was concluded.

19.—Munday. Robert Nelson came in to shop and through my importunacie was preveild with to let me understand the words [which] ware usd in stanching bloud, which is privatly usd amongst countrie persons, and not publickly knowen; and the words are to be seriously said 3 times togather, and so hath beene usd to stanch bloud, said 3 times togather:

> There was a Babe in Bethlem borne
> And christiand in the water of flem[91] Jorden;
> The water it was both wild and wood,[92]
> The child it was both meeke and goode—
> Stanch bloud in God's namme.

See this three times togather.

21.—Wedenesday. I was with John Potter and Tho. Harison att Tankerfeild's with the Harthman[93] that came to view Harthes in Ashton, and spent 4d.

24th.—I was this night with Mathew Raphes and John Hasleden in Joshua Naylor's on purpose to take a house for Joshua and we did take a house of Mathew Raphes.' On this night I saw a comett in the aire, a starr with a traine along with it.[94]

28.—Wedensday. I was envited to supper to Roger Naylor's and went.

29.—Thursday. Att night I went with William Hasleden to be all night att Thomas Heyes', and in the other morneinge I came home.

JENUERY, 1665

1.—I went to Leigh, and Schoole Master had gotten me leave to goe with hime to Mr. Woods' to be all night, but I refusd to goe for this time. Att noone my sister Ellin came to me in the church yard and we went, both of us, to my father and mother's grave and stayd awhile, and both wept. Went to my sister's, Katherin's, and we had 2d. in Ale and so parted. I went into church and there was some christenings, and I went out againe, for my Master's son was to come home with me, and dayes ware short, so I resolved to come homme.

2.—Munday. I went to the funeralle of Jane Potter, John Potter's daughter, of Lilly Lane, who was this day interred at Winwick, and att our comeinge home I was with John Potter of Ashton and James Low and some others, and we went togather into a house cald Spoiler's, in Neawton; spent 4d. and so came home. When I came home Thomas Tickle was come out of Reinford with John Hasleden, and was att John Jenkinson's drinkeinge. They sent for me and I went, but it cost me nothinge, for Raph and John spent, either of them, 12d.

6.—Friday. I went to Beinforlonge, and John Jenkins' wife with me.

8.—Lord's day. Att noone I went home with Robert Rosbothome to dinner, and this night Thomas Smith and I went togather to John Taylor's in Goleborne and heard Mr. Woods preach, and we had a sacrament. We came home this night.

9.—Munday. I was sent to the funerall of my brother's child, cald Raph. I [sic] dyd att Tho. Gerard's house in Windle, and was buryd att St. Ellin this same day.

10.—Tusday. Tho. Tickle came to me out of Reinford to go with hime to old Mr. Woods, who was att John Robinson's. He would receive sacrament. I went with hime, but all was done before we came, and we stayd all night there.

14.—Saturday. Thomas Smith and I went to younge Mr. Woods' in Atherton, where he livd with his wife in Gyles Greene's house. As we went we cald of John Hampson in Hindley, who brought us to Mr. Woods' house. After I had beene in house John and I went to Bent, where Mr. Woods was, and John and I stayd awhile, then parted.

15th.—We all went to Houghton chappell and heard Mr. Lever[95] preache. Att noone John Hampson tooke me home with hime to dinner. The next day we intended home, but Mr. Woods would not suffer us, but all afternoon we shufled att table[96] in Bent. There was Tho. Moxon and I and Peter Twisse playd with Mr. Woods and his partners. We beat them. The other day we came home; Anne Woods and Mr. Woods' maid came with us, and att Ashton we tooke them into Ale house and promisd them to come to them att Widow Clarke's in Windle; but I could not.

29th.—Lord's day. Henry Gerrard sent to mee to procure hime a man to go to Lancer [?] and thence to London, which I did. I get John Jenkinson and this afternoone I wente with hime to Beinforlonge; but Henry Gerard was not att home, and it was suposd he had gotten one.

FEBRUERY, 1665

8.—Wedensday. John Naylor's wife of Edg Greene sent for me thither. They had buryd a lad cald Joseph day before.

9.—Thursday. I went to Blackly Hurst to the funeralle of Mr. Thomas Blakeburne, who was buryd att Winwick.

10.—Friday. Emm Potter and I fell out, and

11.—Saturday, Being in a sad Fitt, I composd these verses Followeing, on thought of somethinge her sister should speake against me on Shrove Tusday night att John Jenkinson's, upon which Emm and I parted:

> Well, I'me content, tho fortune on me frowne,
> God will me raise, tho the world would cast me downe,
> And I with patiance will their mallice bear
> Who seeke to defame me—nay, do curse and swear
> And lye in oposition what they've said.
> But vengeance will att last light on their head;
> Let world say best and worst: all's one to me,
> In time my quarrelle will revenged be.
> Till then I'll waite and onely seeke to God
> That Hee'le be pleasd t' remove this flicting rod,
> And I doe hope that I shall live to see
> Myself inlargd and freed frome callumnie.
> And they that are the acters of my greefe
> May they cry out and yet find no releife.
> But this I wish not: O, that they might be
> Preservd from all such kind of miserie.

This day my old father Stirrope came to towne and movd me to go alonge with hime to Gawther's. I did. He spent his 6d. on me.

15.—Wedensday. I went to Beinforlonge to Anne Greinsworthe to set downe accounts for her.

19.—Lord's day. I went to Winwick to see John Hasleden's love.

26.—Lord's day. I went to Winwick; there was no preachinge att Ashton.

27th.—Munday. Mr. Robt. Greinsworth came from London and cald on me and forced me to go with hime to Beinforlonge; so I gat hime to gat John Jenkins to come with me, because it was night, and I would come. So John and I went and stayd till 12 clock in night drinkeing, and afterwards we came home, and

28.—Tusday, I was sicke all day, but ere night the Lord restord me.

MARCH, 1665

2.—Thursday. Henry Houghton came to me to have me make a lease for hime of his house, between Mr. Byrome de Byrome and hime.

3.—Friday. I went to his house to buy a heifer in calve, and I bought her for 39s., and he was to keape her a month.

14th.—Tusday. Henry Houghton came to me and William Crouchley and had me to go with them to Parr Hall[97] to seale lease to Mr. Byrom. He seald it, and Mr. Edward Byrom and his two Brothers that ware distrected went and brought us to an Ale house, where we sat drinkeinge a good while. Then we passed for homme, and Att Ashton I mett with some Leigh people that ingagd me to be with them, and I was with theme.

24th.—Friday. My Master came to towne, and he had told me that he had heard many things of me and wishd me for my good to be cautious. He spoke very loveingly to me, and I was efraid before he came, lest he would have beene angry.

26.—Lord's day. I went to Leigh, and John Chadocke and I walked after the Brookeside in Slate feilds att noone, discoursing about my effaires and my Master. Att our returne into Towne I went into George Norris's house to old Mr. Woods, who was there, and stayd awhile; then went into church, and Mr. Crampton[98] preached and I was glad of it.

28.—Tusday. I was envited and went to John Hasleden's mariage att Winwick; was his manne.

APRILLE, 1665

2.—Lord's day. John Hasleden and I went to the Lees beyond Holland to heare Mr. Baldwin[99] preach, and att Hugh Worthington's in Holland we ware to meet with Thomas Tickle and other Reinford men, which we did and stayd drinkeing of 8d., and so went to one Mr. Lawrance Hallewelle's, where Mr. Baldwin was, and he preacht in the forenoone and intended to preach in the afternoone, but we ware prevented with some women that came into house, and some of them ware papists, so we ware forced to come home before later sermon was preached; and att Holland we stayd drinking of 12d. and then parted home, but Thomas Tickle payd it.

3.—Munday. Mr. Banister de Banke[100] came through Ashton, being slaine att Forest of Dellimore, being accompenide with store of gentry. Att sunn setting this eveninge Ann Johnson departed this life.

5.—Wedensday. I went to Standish to the funeralle of Anne Johnson, and I came into the church when Mr. Bowker was preachinge, for it was a day of Humilietion For the King's navy.[101] Set out att after she was interred and was come into house, where we dranke and saw how they intended to serve us who ware come out of Ashton, with every one a loafe.[102] John Potter and I ware som what Hungery and angry. We tooke fleight to Wiggan to Eles Leighe's and there refreshed our selves.

11.—Tusday. I went to the funeralle of Grace Gerard to Winwicke, who was there interred.

16.—Saturday. I went with John Hasleden and his wife into Reinford to Henry Sephon, and

18th.—Munday. We came home togather.

23.—Lord's day. I went to Leigh.

28.—Friday. I was in greefes all day in consideracion of my charge, for fear shop should not answer my Master's expectation, being now to be cast up. But my trust is in the Lord, who never failes those who trust in hime.

29.—Saturday. Peter Leyland came to towne and wishd me to go bringe hime towards home, and in William Knowe's feild, cald Horse Head under Banke, we sat down, and he told me his trouble in regard of his daughter's distemper, which was falling sicknes,[103] and his two sonnes, that the one was void of a callinge and the other weake and infirme, and amidst our talke we both fell fast esleepe.

30.—Lord's day. Mr. Pilkington, person of Crosson,[104] preacht here, and att night I went downe to hime. He was att Thomas Naylor's and [I] envited hime to take a flaggon. We went to Thomas Leeche's and stayd awhile and so parted.

MAY, 1665

1.—Munday. This morneinge I went with Thomas Harison with a sterke to Lodge to have her scord.[105]

2.—Tusday. My Brother with his wife came with his beasts, removeing out of Windle into Houghton to Dazy Hillocke to Peter Ryland's house, he that was the sequestrator, and I brought them towards Houghton, and I was exceedingly troubled in my mind for my poor Brother.

7.—Lord's day. Mr. Byrom came to towne. Mr. Bowker preachd, and att night John Jenkinson and I went with Mr. Byrom to bringe hime towards home.

11th May.—My Master came to Ashton and told me I must come home and bid me to set all things in order. This was sad newes, but it's good to submitt to God in his verious providences.

15.—Munday night. I went to be all night att John Robbinson's. There was old Mr. Woods and Mr. Martindale.[106]

16.—Tusday. I went to Beinforlonge, and this night I was in a sad condition by reason of Ann Taylor's comeinge to Ellin Harison and tellinge her storys of me, [in] so much as Emm Potter beinge att Halsalle, I was almost intendinge to have gone in night. I was sadly troubled and was att this time very vehement[107] in effection towards her.

17.—Wedensday. I went about twelve aclocke att noone to meet her, and upon the Brow this side Orrell Moor, short of the barne that stands by it selfe in the vally there, in a ditch I sate where I might see all the moor over, desireing to see my wished sight. It raind, and after I was almost tyred in waiteing I resolved to go down Brow towards Barne, and in goeinge I mett with Devid Pendlebery, an Ashton man, homewards; so I asked hime wheither he would go spend this 1d. att Skenneing John's, who said he would. We ware no sooner gotten into house and had a flaggon, but Mr. Leigh, schoole Master of Ashton,[108] came in. It was a rainy day and my expectations was frustrate. That troubled me much, so we stayd 2 or 3 flaggons and then parted, and I came home and she was come before me and was undrest; but notwithstanding Taylor had done her indeavor to incense her against me, yet it was in vaine and I was very glad to see her.

28.—Lord's day. I went to Leigh and had a litle Hare for children. Att noone I went to John Chadocke's and he and I went awalking and discourseing about me: what I should doe in answer to my selfe, betweene me and my Master. Att night my Dame would have me take mare home with me, and litle Thomas behind me, so we did. Litle Thomas was troubled with sores, and they would have me to go with hime to Markland's the other morneing, which we did, and left mare we rid off att widow Clarke's till we returnd backe from Markland's. So att our returne to Ashton I went to see how he could ride, and brought hime to further end of Towne Greene, and so left hime.

JUNE, 1665

1.—Thursday. I went with Sarah Jenkinson's brotherley[109] and brother to Henry Frances in Pemberton to see the burneing well,[110] and we had 2 eggs, which was ... [illegible] by no materiall fire. We returnd backe to Watt's of Whitleige Greene, and there I had information that Robert Pendleberry had sent for ribbininge[111] to marle pitt, which causd my hast to shop, and thence to Robert's.

3.—Saturday night. James Jenkins and I went all up and downe to find John Jenkins, who was suposd to be drownd, but att 12 clocke in night we found hime fast esleepe amidst Town Feild.

5.—Munday. Daniell Chadocke was come to towne to Meete Mr. Taylor, who was come over and gone to his unkle Stirrope. We went, Daniell Chadocke, John Jenkinson, and I, to Goleborne Copp,[112] and sent to Mr.

Taylor to have hime come thither, and when we came we went to the Alley and playd att bowles; and annon Mr. Potter came, and Mr. Widowes, John Jenkins, and I beat Mr. Potter, Mr. Taylor, and Mr. Chadocke in each of them 4d. in Ale.

6.—Tusday. I went to Warington to buy some ware I wanted and to pay some mony, and Mr. Worrell was very respectfull to me, and comforted me very much for dayes to come, and so did Mr. Scofeild.

7.—Wedensday. I was sent for to Beinforlonge to Anne Greinsworth, and went.

11.—Lord's day. In the afternoone I went to Neawton to hear Mr. Taylor preach. I was very pensive and sad att this time in consideracion of my condition in this world. But God is the rocke to which I hold, and the waters of consolation is still distilled frome hime, amidst the greatest discouragments.

13.—Tusday. I was sent for to Beinforlonge, and I went.

18.—Lord's day. I went to Wiggan and heard Mr. Kenion,[113] pastor of Prestwidge, most excelantly preach.

19.—I went to Leigh and was ill wett.

22.—Thursday. I went to Leigh and had borowed six pound for my Master against Chester faire.

24.—Saturday. In the afternoone Mr. Leanders came and wild me to goe to Goleborne Copp to bowle, and I see a game or two bowld and came home againe.

25.—Lord's day. Mr. Taylor preacht att Ashton. I went to Beinforlonge this night to make streight Anne's accounts, for she was effraid her brother would come from London.

27.—Tusday. I went to John Robbinson's, For his daughter, widow Jaxon, had envited me upon a privat account to ecqueint me of some private buisnes, and this afternoone I had spent with Mr. Bowker, vicker of Standish, and Mr. Leanders; and after I had parted with them I went towards John Robinson's and it was a very rainy eveninge. I went to Symon Marsh and bought 1 dozen of sythes and so returned to John Robinson's and was all night, and the matter she had to ecqueint me was that if I ware leafe Mr. Martindale had and could provide a good wife for me, a women in Chester, his one sisterley, Major Jollye's[114] fil, [who] hath 120 li. to her portion. I was glad of the buisnes and had some hopes of freedom frome my Master.

28.—Wedensday. Betime in the morneinge I came home, and Mr. Bowker sent for me, and we ware togather a certaine time.

29th.—Thursday. I was with the white smiths[115] of Ashton, and made an agreement For them to goe to counsell with about their trade. This night I went to Robert Rosbothom's and was there all night, and Richard Orme askd me to make a pair of Indentures and two bonds, and he gave me directions about them. I was at this time sadly troubled concerneinge Mrs. Rosthorne's death, who dyed att Bold Hall,[116] where she was borne, and then caried to Lodge[117] in Chowbent, and upon the 31th June was interred att Leigh. She was caried dead from Bold to Atherton in a horse litter.

JULY, 1665

1.—Lord's day. Mr. Henmar preached att Ashton,

and att night Tho. Smith and I went to old John Robbinson's and there repeated both sermons.

6.—Friday. Anne Barrow sent for me. She livd with her sister, Margret Naylor, on Edg Greene, and there I repeated Mr. Henmar's sermons.

11.—Wedensday. I went to Leigh.

30.—Lord's day. I went to Wiggan. Joshua Naylor and John Hasleden went along with me, and when we came to Eles Leighe's we stayd and had each a cupp of ale, and then I left them drinkeing and I went into church, and att noone when I came out they ware gone homewards. I was all this time in expectation of my Master, to come cast up shop, and he came not, which troubled me very much.

AUGUST, 1665

6.—Lord's day. Edward Hayhurst, junior, of Chowbent sent For me this morneinge and wishd me to goe with hime to Denton Green. He wood Tho. Holland's daughter, and I promisd hime I would. He hyred me a horse and we went to Denton Greene to one Darbishire's ale house, and sent for her, but she was gone to church and the wife sent for us; so we went and stayd there till she came home and ware much made of; but we had a rainy eveninge home.

8.—Tusday. Richard Orme came, and I went with hime and John Potter into Windle to seale Indentures I had made for to bynd Henry Orme prentice to Josiah Clarke, sadler. When he was bound, we rid upp to Denton Greene, For John Potter, I thanke hime, let me ride behind hime; and att Denton Green we stayd and playd three games of bowles and spent each 2d. And so we parted and ware ill wett.

12.—I went with Mr. Launders to Goleborn Copp and playd att bowles.

13.—Lord's day. Edmund Hayhurst came and enjoined me to go to Mr. Sorowcold to move hime to goe act the buisnes for him for a marige.

14.—Betime this morneing I went to Mr. Sorowcold upon that buisnes. Att my comeing home I went to Winwick to the funerall of a child of Josiah Naylor, and John Potter and I went with Thomas Lyon to Hoornes Greene, where ere we parted there was some differance betweene Thomas Lyon and Darbishire, who ware ingagd in a game of Bowles and could not agree; and in Parlor, where we ware, was Mr. Mather, an attorney that defended Thomas Lyon's case and provokd us to much passion. But John Potter and I ware for peace, and this Mather puts us all in one and intends to sue us.

23 day.—I went to Warington and John Potter, too, on purpose to know his pleasure, and att home att Thomas Kerfoote's I cald. He and his wife had spoke much for me, so I gat them to go along with me, which they did, and Mather said he would be civill with me—that was all. I went to seeke John Potter and found hime not till I was just parting with towne, where I found hime in Mather's sister's house; so we went to his hot house[118] and spent 2d., and he let me ride behinde hime home, and we ware both exceedingly hungry, and we cald att Heapy's in Neawton and whiles we ware eateing and drinking we had almost faln out about presbittery and episcopecie.

20.—Lord's day. I was with young Mr. Woods att old John Robinson's, and I was all night. Mr. Woods preached and he would not let me passe home, and the other day he came to towne with me.

27.—Lord's day. I went to Wigin, Thomas Smith with me, and we cald of Robert Rosbothom, and he and his wife went along with us. I told Thomas Smith my greevences about Emm and me fallinge out, and her sister; so we cast[119] that Thomas should come on Thursday after to Tankerfeild's and send for Emm, and there conclude a peace. Att night Robert and wife ware gone home and Thomas and I followed, and we cald att Adamson's of Goose Greene, and spent 3d. So we parted to Robert's, where they ware att super. We stayd super, and so came homme.

30.—Wedensday. I received a letter from Thomas Johnson of Laverpoole and a lad with a horse, where he desired me to go with the lad and pay James Boydells for caridge of wine and receive it for Thomas, which I did, and when I was upon Louton Comon I tooke horse and went to Leigh and gat some goods, and so passed away back againe.

SEPTEMBER, 1665

3.—Lord's day. I went to Billinge Chappell in the afternoone with John Potter and others, and we went and cald on Henry Birchalle in the Feilds, and spent each 2d., and so went to chappelle. When eveninge service was done Mr. Blakeburne envited me into house, but I could not goe, but desired excuse. We came backe againe to Henry Birchalle and stayd awhile and so came for homme.

12.—Tusday. In the afternoone I went to John Robbinson's; there was a privat day and a sacrament. Old Mr. Woods preached. I came as he was preaching, and

I receivd the sacrement: the Lord sanctifie it unto me.
There was Mary Barkon there, to whom I had some
thoughts, too, and intended to send Tho. Smith to speake
my buisnes. This night Thomas Smith was made up to
Eles Lealand in old John Robinson's chamber.

23 —Wedensday. My Master had sent me a very
shrewd messege by Peter Higson, and I framed a letter
and gat Thomas Smith to go speake my buisnes. He
went on St. Mathew's day[120] and my Master was sore
displeasd.

29.—Friday. I went with Edward Hayhurst to Denton
Greene; he hired me a horse.

OCTOBER, 1665

8.—Lord's day night. Thomas Smith asked me to go
with hime to Peter Lealand's, which I did. Sarah Hasleden
asked me to come to their house, which I did, and
there was a Rosted goose and I eate my super.

9.—Munday. I went with Thomas Smith to Winwick
to his mariege with Eles Lealand. Att night I was envited
per old Peter to goe home with them, which I did,
and stayd super.

13.—Friday night. I went with old William Hasleden
and his horses with two strangers to Laverpoole within
night, meerely out of my one mind.

23.—Munday. I went into Haddock to seaverall
houses to gett monyes, but I gat none.

30th.—Tusday. I went with John Potter, Richard
Asmull, John Darbishire to Winwick to meet Mr. Mather,
one that threatend to sue us and for which I was under

great trouble, but when we came thither he was att Neawton att Rothell's; so we all went thither and sent for hime. But his demands was so extreordinerie that we all came home very sad.

NOVEMBER, 1665

1.—Wedensday. I went to Leigh, and when I came into Towne I found Raph Jenkins in the stocks[121] and a fire upon the Crosse by hime; he had beene all night there. Att my comeinge home I gate a horse and resolved to goe to Winstanly to speake and move Mr. Blakeburne to be my freind about Mather's buisnes. We came downe to Humphry Atherton's, sate in the parlour by the fire, and talked a great while, of every thing some thinge, and he showd very great respect, and he would doe what lye in him to doe for me.

5.—Lord's day. I went to Billinge chappell and heard Mr. John Blakeburne preach. He shewd me a letter he had receivd from Mather, and he promisd to reverse the buisnes that terme, and Mr. John told me he would not be wantinge in any thinge for me. I dined att John Cowly's.

7.—Tusday night. I went to Thomas Smith's; he lived att Cooke's house near to Robert Rosbothom's house. I was there all night with hime. The other morneinge Thomas and I went to his fatherley's, Peter Lealand, to get hime to goe to Watt's house to see if he could take it for them.

14.—Tusday. My Master came and I was in a sad sorowfull estate for fear of being under hand. My Master profferd to let me have goods and to free me.

17.—Friday. I rid before Sarah Hasleden to Leigh to

see my accounts. I was chargd with 205 li. and I had
profited 48 li. I was glad then. I went with Sarah to
Hugh Hindley's, for his daughter was lyeing in. Att our
returne againe my Master was proffering shop to me,
and I excepted of it, and I was to pay in such time. So
I was made free; tho I was very sorowfulle, yet my trust
is in God.

20th.—Munday. I went to Warington and bought
ceronce[122] and other comodities.

14.—My Master came and cast up shop and thought
I had beene far behind hand, but on the 17th day I and
Sarah Hasleden went to Leigh, and I went to perfect all
accounts, and I had gained my Master 48 li. in a yeare
and a halfe, and I was very glad. I went with Sarah to
Hugh Hindley's, for his daughter was lying in, but when
I came to Leigh againe, my Master profferd me to trust
me for the goods in Ashton, and to give me my time,
which I excepted of. God hath beene with me hitherto:
his name be glorifide.

DECEMBER, 1665

20.—I went to Leigh and gat my Master to let me have
some comodities I wanted, which he did, and sent his
sone to bring them me. I was att this time sadly troubled
for fear of miscaryinge, and knew not how to get cloth
and things. Yet God raised up freinds for me, for a
Yorkeshire man came through towne and profferd to let
me have cloth for three months.

21.—I went to Warrington and Thomas Peake was
very earnest with me to have me be a journy man for
hime in Laverpoole, which I danyd. I bought some
comodities upon trust of Mr. Worrell; so came home.

26.—Tusday. I went with John Potter and Thomas Harison to Manchester. We ware up very early and gat to Boothes towne by day; came [to] Earlome's and spent each 2d. apeece, for I begun to be very feeble. And then we came to Manchester, and in the first place we went to church and lookd about us, and anon the quristers came and we stayd morneinge prayer. I was exceedinglie taken with the mellodie. Then we three, haveing each seavrall buisnes to do, and goeinge to get John Potter's buisnes done first: I showd Thomas Harrison Mr. Sandiforth's, where he was to doe his buisnes, and he and I went and enquird for hime. As soone as he see me [he] very kindlie tooke me in and would not let me passe till I had dined with hime, and so did Thomas, too. But this while we had lost John Potter, and made much labour to find hime, and whiles we ware afinding hime I gat my buisnes perfected with Mr. Howham. But when we had found John Potter he was very angry att us. Then we went altogather to a house John Jenkins brought us to, where we ware troubled with fowle sheets all night. But all this day we could not perfect nothing of John Potter's buisnes, which was to be done with one Robert Johnson, a draper, who was out of town; but in far of night we went to his house, when we heard of his comeinge home by John Hopwood, to whom we ware ingagd much to, and gat his buisnes done.

27.—We sat out of Manchester, and John Potter was not well, and besides, he over went Thomas and me to Earlom's and never gave us word, all which troubled me exceedinglie in my mind. But we all came to Earlom's and there we ware mery, and thence we came to Leigh and at widow Raniker's we stayd and spent each of us 2d. apeece. From thence we came home, but by the way had a litle unhapy discourses about religion, as too of we have been overtaken with too much passion; for each of us ware of differant judgments and each would vindicate his one way, and many times fall into an exceedinge passion, tho it never occasiond us to love the lesse, which I often marked as a providence of God; for I received so many singular favours from them as causd me to love them entirely. Att our comeing into Tho. Harison's we found an old man and his wife, that Thomas was ingagd too. We went to Ale house and ware very mery togather.

30.—Saturday. Robt. Rosbothom sent for me; Mr. Woods was come to his house, and I went, and Mr. Woods preached. I lay att Thomas Smith's, who lived then att Cooke's house.

JENUERY, 1666

1.—Munday. I went to Nicholas Croft to bid hime fatch the cow.

2.—Tusday. I went a hunteinge and the hare tooke into the rapits' holes, and I was exceedingly wearied.

3.—Wedensday. I went to Leigh to speake to Mr. Swift, who was come and gone againe. I was sadlie troubled. I came away by my sister Ellin's and stayd awhile, and so came to Richard Orme's, for I should have stayd there all night. Richard was not att home and so I came home.

4.—Thursday. I gat Tho. Harison to goe along with me to Peter Lealand's, Hadocke Wood, to looke att a chest for me, which I was to buy.

10.—Wedensday. I went a hunteinge awhile and then came home.

15.—Munday. I hired Tho. Leech's horse and rid to Standish on purpose to buy me a suite of brown shagge,[123] but there was none. I came backe to Wiggin and stayd to speake with Mr. Pilkinton about mony that a servent of his owd my Master. I had the compenie of one Hugh Toppinge of Warington, who told me there was the head of some Christian lay bare to publicke view above ground, and that it was charitie to bury it, which I said I would doe.

16.—Tusday. I went to bury it. It lay in the High Lane as one goes to Barlyman's, just att the crosse cawsaw.[124] I caried it in my hands to the dungeon's slift in the Town Feild, and there buryd it; I digd the hole with my fingers. It was suposd to have beene a Scott, and there slaine when Duke Hamleton invaded England.[125]

17.—Wedensday. I went to Warington and payd Richard Worrell all that I owd hime. I bought me a new Hatt and stockins. Came to Neawton and there spent 4d.

19.—Friday. I went to the Funerall of old Mrs. Birch, beinge envited by John Jenkins.

23.—John Jenkinson desired me to goe with his child to Winwick to stand as a godfather. Mr. Bowker had faild and could not come, so he intreated me to go with hime, which I did, and he went into Clarke's att after the christeninge and spent 3s. Then we went to widow Barker's and we spent other 3s. But it was a very rugged night and darke, yet John and I came home.

FEBRUERIE, 1666

2.—Friday. I went with John Potter and his wife to his wive's sister's, who lived att a place called Lawnes, and we ware much made of. Att after diner we went up to Holland to Thomas Prescott's and ware mery, and then to Humphry Naylor's and stayd awhile, and so came to Lawnes againe, where we all of us supt; and then John

Potter and I came home, and honest Thomas Birchall would not leave us, but came home with us. But James Low stayd all night there and left us, which was not well taken. Att this time there was one Gaskell, who owed [sic] Tower Hill house above the Lawnes, had hanged hime selfe.

3.—Saturday. Emm and I ware exceedinglie falne out, which greeved me sore, and she was gone with Ann Taylor towards Goleborne Coppe, and I gat Mathew Turton to go with me, and we went and tooke them in the Copp house. I sat down with them, but shee would not be movd. I spent 12d. and was more greeved then before.

4.—Lord's day. I went with John Potter to Billinge Chappell, and att noone we came to Henry Birchall's to diner, where we stayd all afternoone and drunke.

5.—Munday. I was sent for to my sister Ellin, who was brought to bed and was likely for death, and when I came to her she was speecchles, which greeved me sore. I stayd all the after noone and att night, after sun go downe, I parted and came home, and about 8 of clock in night when I was gone she dyd.

6.—Tusday. I went to the Funerall of my dear sister, and her child was christend the same day she was buryd att Winwicke, per Mr. Potter. Mr. Watt came to the Funerall to acompenie me, which I was ingagd for. My sister's child was namd Roger.

10.—Saturday. Mr. Bowker came to Ashton, and I went to bringe hime to Nicholas Burscoe's house, For there he was all night, and in the way we Fell out extremelie about religion, but one

11th.—Lord's day, In the morneinge, when he came

H

to Ashton backe againe, he sent for me and we ware freinds.

18.—Lord's day. I went to Winwick with John Potter. We came home att noone. Mr. Potter would have me to diner.

19.—Munday. I was sadly troubled in my thoughts by reason of the debts I did owe and for fear lest I should miscary. Now the Lord help me and be my helper till death and att death; now the Lord bring me out of these troubles in His good time.

MARCH, 1666

6.—Tusday. Att night I went to Robert Rosbothom's and was there all night.

7.—Wedensday. I went to John Robinson's and was all night.

8.—Thursday. I went to Mr. John Blakeburn to Winstanly to treate with hime about Mather's buisnes, who had sent to hime, so he sent to me to have me come to hime; and concerneinge this buisnes I was much ingagd to honest Mr. Blakeburne. I envited Mr. Blakeburne down to Humphry Winstanly's; we went. I told hime they had assessed me in Ashton for a personell state, and I had none, so he told me what course to take, which I did. After we had drunke awhile I parted. Att my comeing to Ashton I resolved to set forward to Leigh and from thence to Light Okes,[126] but when I came to Leigh Sir Henry Slater was in towne. I gat my Master to go with me to hime, and so ecqueinted hime with my buisnes. He movd me to come the day ensuing, and it should be done. I parted and went from Leigh to Mr. James Woods' house, who lived then att James Dawson's in Atherton and was in a weake condition. We ware a litle mery the other day; I stayd till noone readinge in the *Booke of Martirs*,[127] and then departed to my brother's, who lived att Ryland's house att Dazy Hillock, and stayd awhile there, and so went to Leigh, where I found Sir Henry Slater and Mr. Rosthorne att Robinson's, and Thomas Naylor, who was Sir Henry's clarke, made great professions of love to me, writt me and order and causd it to be signd by the two Justices, and would have nothinge for his labour, so I came home. I found the Lord a helper of me in my distresses; His holy name be praised.

12.—Munday. I was advisd to give this order I had gotten from the Justices to the Constable, which I did, and went with the Constable to Thomas Naylor's, because he had causd me to be layd.[128]

14.—Wedensday. I went to Warrington to pay some monys I owd to Scholefeild.

18.—Lord's day. Emm and I fell out this eveninge. I went to old John Robinson's, was all night. Old Mr. Woods was there and preached, and there was Mary Barton there all night, and I intended to send to her, which I did. Edmund Winstanly's wife the other day . . .

25th March 1666. I went, being Lord's day, to the Funerall of old Allin's wife, who was interred att Winwick. I was with John Potter and Thomas Harison with some others, and we spent 3d. apeece att after the funerall, and thence came to Rothwell's in Neawten, and spent each other 3d. beside, and so we parted home. I was ill all night, but the Lord had mercie on me the other morneinge.

27.—Tusday. I went to Laverpoole to buy comodities. I light of Mr. Reynolds, Sir William's steward, who enjoined me to come to Mr. Christian's to hime. We spent most of the afternoone in drinkeing. I parted and came to Mr. Johnson's shop, where I gatе some buisnes done, and in the doeinge of my affaires I mett with Mr. Swift, whome I intended to go too. He lived in Chester; he was a Bristoll marchant and traded in Bristoll goods. I was to goe to hime the next morneinge, which I did, and went up to his chamber where he lyed and he causd a potle[129] of butt end [?] ale to come up, so I gat my buisnes done and then set forward for Ashton, and made Highton my way. Cald of Mr. Low, the vicar, and we went to the Clarkes' house and ware merry awhile, and then I came home.

30.—Friday night. I was all night att Robert Rosbothom's. This night Raph Low, son of Dame End, hanged him selfe in shippon[130] before beasts.

APRIL, 1666

13th.—Good Friday. John Hasleden's wife was under the pangs of child birth, and they sent for me to pray by her, which I did. Att this time I was in great sadnes, not knoweing what to doe.

16.—Munday. I went to Leigh to pay some monys to my Master, and he was out towne. William Dewnelle was in towne about his daughter's mariage with Mr. Chadock; he sent for me and I rid behind hime home. The remainder of this month to the 14th May I was sadly efficted with pains, but the Lord restord me.

MAY, 1666

14.—Munday. I went to Robert Rosbothom's and was all night.

28.—Munday, was the first day I could say I was well, so that it pleased God to eflict me for 5 weekes just. The last day of this month I was but weake and I went with Joshua Naylor to Whitleige Greene on purpose to recreate my selfe, and Watt's wife made much over me. Mr. Sorowcold's man came for me. Att my comeinge home I had a booke of Mr. Ambrose's, late minister of Preston, who att the end of his booke had these psalms in meeter:

Psalm 100

All men of mortell birth
That dwell in all the earth,
O make a noise to God with joys
And serve the Lord with mirth.

Oh come before His throne
With singeinge every one,
For certainly the Lord most high,
Even He is God alone.

He made us and not we,
Not we our selves, but Hee;
His folke and flock and pasture stock
He made us for to be.

With praise come to His gate
And to His courts relate
His laud and fame, and bless his name,
His honor celebrate.

For God is good For ever,
His mercie Faileth never;
His truth doth last all ages past
And constant doth persever.

Psa. 108, 1 part

O God, I fix my hart,
My glory bears apart,
And as my tongue, so shall my songe
Praise Thee with musick's art.

Wake, harpe and psaltery,
Right early wake will I;
Thy praises, Lord, will I record,
The people standing by.

I'le praise Thee with my songe
The nations all amonge;
To heavens high, to clouds of sky
His truth and mercies throng.

Exalted be Thy name
Above the heavens' frame;
Let earth below the trumpet blow
Of Thy renowned fame.

Psal. 150

Praise, praise the Lord most high
Within His sanctuary;
In topmost tower of His great power
With praise Hime magnifie.

Praise Hime for acts renownd
With excelancie crownd;
Acording to His greatnes do
Praise Hime with trumpet sound.

O praise Hime chearfuly
With harp and psalterie,
And let the dance His praise advance,
And timbrals mallodie.

Praise Hime with joint consents
Of stringed instruments;
The organs bringe, loud cimbals ringe:
Each one His praise presents.

High-sounding Cimbals ringe,
Let everie breathinge thinge
The praise record of this great Lord
And haleluiah singe.

JUNE, 1666

1.—Friday and Saturday. Both these days I was in a sadded condition in my thoughts by reason of my great debts; but my hope is in God that He will helpe me out.

3.—Lord's day. I went to Billinge chappell to hear Mr. Blakeburne, and he was glad to se me recovered. He tooke me into Humphrey Cowly's and spent 6d. on me, and then I walked downe to Blackly Hurst, and so parted.

8.—Friday. I went to bringe John Jenkins' wife's old Cock towards Winwick. I intended to go to Winwick, bit I found my selfe unable and soe returned home.

14.—Thursday. I went to Whitleige Greene with John Potter and Thomas Harison and lost 2d. att bowles, and so came home.

20th.—Wednesday. Att night I went to old John Robinson's and was there all night, and widow Jackson promisd me her horse to go to Chester on.

24.—Lord's day. I went att noone into Abram to Anne Taylor's, and Emme Potter was there, but shee would not admitt me to speake to her, soe I had Thomas

Hesketh with me and we went to the Brinne and cald att Beinforlonge of younge Mr. Gerard, and he accomodated us with drinke; so returninge thankes we parted and came to Brinne to se some worke tooles that he had hid, and so we came home.

28th.—Thursday. I sat Forwards for Chester. Widow Jaxon lent me a horse, and near Fradsam bridge[131] the horse halted extreamly. I alighted of and puld a single spikeinge out of his foote and the horse did a litle halt. I gat well to Chester by God's helpe; went to Mr. Swift to whom I payd ten pound. I lay att Dragon. I went to hear organs and the quiristers, and I was so wearie as I went in the midle of their service.

29th.—Friday. I sat homewards, haveing, as I thought, well done my buisnes, and att Warington I lighted and stayd awhile and so came home, but withall mett in the way Mr. John Potter, ill tipled, whom I did not leave till I came home.

JULY, 1666

1.—Lord's day. The schoole master of Ashton came and intreated me to goe with hime to Standish to speake to Mr. Bowker to be his freind for the obtaininge of a schoole near Preston. I went with hime, being bound in charitie. It rained; notwithstandinge, we went, and when we came to Standish he was in one Thomas Smith's, and he sent for me. We went to hime and att noone we dined with hime att Thomas Taylor's, in the Brick house, and he promisd to doe what in hime did lye.

2.—Munday. Mr. Hopwood and his wife ware att John Jenkinson's and sent for me. I went and spent me 4d., which was contrarie to Mr. Hopwood's mind.

3.—Tusday. Em Potter had ecqueinted me that she was told that my mother bore me a bastard. I conceived who had spoken it for to be Elizebeth Potter, and she was att this presant in towne, so I sifted it out and found she was the women, and she told me that William Morris had expressed it. I resolved for Leigh and intended to be the death of William and intended to call of my brother and have hime with me, but I was prevented, for I cald att Heapy's, and there was John Chadock came by and Mr. Holecroft. I rid behind John Chadock to Lowton Smithy's and so came to Leigh to Izibell Grundie's, cald for a chamber and sent for William Morris. He came, and Thomas Insworth with hime. I wishd hime to give place awhile; when he was gone I to Will and buffeted hime very mery. Nicholas Mather came up and was very vehamant against me. We parted that house and went to widow Ranicar's. I spent me 12d., so came and did lye with Clarke. The other morneinge I went to doe some buisnes with my Master, and I told hime my case; he was ill troubled att it and counseld me for my good, so I came home with a sad spirit and I cald of my brotherley, Henry Houghton, and he was gone to be maried, so I parted.

16.—Munday. I went with John Potter and Joshua Naylor to Henry Birchall's to see a Cock to fight. I was ill troubled in my mind that I went.

28.—Lord's day. I went to Wiggan on purpose to hear the Bishop, for I was som what discomposd in mind by reason of Em Potter and me Fallinge out, and I went to shake it of me, and I heard the Bishop. He preached against atheisticalnes.

AUGUST, 1666

1.—Wedensday. I went to Neawton faire[132] in the afternoone and mett with my Master.

5.—Lord's day. I went to Billinge Chappelle to hear Mr. Blakeburne. I went in the afternoone.

9th.—I went to Warrington and payd 52 shillings, where I owd it up and downe.

13.—I went to Wiggan, but came too late to hear the Bishop preach.

15.—I went to Prescott, being Wedensday, and I went upon an idle occasion. God forgive me.

16.—I was pensive and sad all day by reason I had heard some thing of Emm's unfaithfulnes to me, and it greeved me very sore.

26.—Lord's day. I went to Wiggan to hear the Bishop preach. I dined with John Naylor att Eles Leighe's. There was buryd behind the great church door, within the church, one Sarjant Lanchshaw. He lived in the Scowles.[133]

24th.—Friday. Being Bartholomew Day I hired a horse and went with Thomas Leech to Crosson. Mr. Pilkington was parson and one Will Harys lived with hime, and he owd I monys, and we went to get it, but found not hime att home. We found Thomas Naylor there and through hime and his son's perswasion we went with them to Chorley; it was the faire. I was no sooner gotten into the Towne but I mett with Robt. Reynolds, and when I was alight he and I went to see a show concerneing the lifes of man from his infancie to old age. We parted, and when I came to receive my horse I wanted a shoo. All I spent was 2d., so I came easily homewards, and amidst Chorly Moor I gat a shoo; came homewards, and in Wiggan Mr. Bowker envited me to Anne Cason's, gave me a part of a botle or two of Rosbary ale, and so I came home.

31.—Thursday. I went to Warrington and att my comeinge home I was not well, yet get home.

SEPTEMBER, 1666

2.—Lord's day. I went with John Potter to Wiggan to hear the bishop, but he was gone to Knowsley, and he had burned 4 or 5 bey[134] of stableinge and shipeninge this morneinge by the carelesnes of the groome, who let the candle burne att his bed's head, and he fell asleepe.

4.—Tusday night. I went to old John Robinson's; was all night. O how comfortable is the comunion of Saints!

18.—Friday. I went with John Potter to Winwick, and Mr. Potter envited me to dinner, and att after prayers—for it was St. Mathew's Day—he went with us into the Springe and we spent 4d., and att night, as we came home, we overtooke Emm and Kenion togather, and I was ill troubled.

19.—Saturday. I went to my brother's into Burton Wood, and on Lord's day morneinge we came for Ashton and cald to se Braidley Hall,[135] which I admir to se so goodly a fabrick lying wast.

OCTOBER, 1666

13th.—Friday. I went with Raph Winstanley and John Potter to the Funeralle of old Mr. Bankes of Winstanley, who was interred att Wiggan. Mr. Bl[a]ke[burne] preached.

16.—Monday. Mr. Blakeburne wishd me to go [with] John Naylor and William Chadocke to see what people would give towards the releife of such needie persons as had sustaind losse by the great fire in London, and to set their names downe, which we did over the one halfe of Ashton.

29th.—I went to Roberts Rosbothom's and was all night.

NOVEMBER, 1666

3d.—Lord's day. I went with John Potter to Winwick, and Mr. Potter envited me to Diner and I went.

27.—Tusday. I went to Leigh and made all things streight with my Master and turned over John Greenhough and Thomas Greenhough to discharge the debt I owd, which my Master assented to. He would have faine concluded me with . . . the debt, but I would not, so he tooke Thomas Greenough's bond with his son John Greenhough bound For all the debt I owd to hime; so he cleard me before John Chadocke in his one shope and before John Greenhough, who came with me home and att Joshua Naylor's spent either 6d.

30th.—Friday—St. Andrewe's Day. I went to Garswood[136] about widow Taylor's buisnes of exchangeinge the lease, and Sir William [137] made a promise per the way between hall and Kitchin that he would speake to his sonn, for he it was that must doe that buisnes.

DECEMBER, 1666

2.—Lord's day. John Potter and I went to Billinge chapell; Mr. Blakeburne preached. It was a cold day and att noone Humphry Cowly's house was so thronged that we could not ataine a fire to sit by, but we sacrificed ourselves ore the twopeny flagone in a cold chamber. All noone there was Henry Birchall with us, the younger. We had each of us a messe a pottage; we spent 3d. apeece.

15.—Saturday. I went to the dolefull funeralle of the reverand Mr. John Blakeburne att Winwick. Mr. Potter preached in a very pethaticall maner out of the 14 Revelations, 1 part of the 13 verse: "Blessed are the dead that dye in the Lord." He in the close of his sermon spoke excelantlie truely, tho mournfullie, in comendation of Mr. John, and indeed the neighborhood sustaine great losse by his death.

16.—Lord's day. I went to the funeralle of Ann Taylor, who was maried to Raph Ashton in Abram, and I went fastinge from home, so at noone, when we had buried the corps and expected acording to custome to have some refreshment and ware a compenie of neighbors sate togather round about a table, as John Poter, Tho. Harison, and others, the Doctor comes and prohibits the filling of any drinke till after prayers; so I came home with Thomas Harison and we expected to have cald att Neawton, but here we ware disapointed. But att last with much vexetion I gat to Ashton with a hungry belly, and honest Thomas Harison and right true harted Ellin, tho hastie, yet all love, did much refresh my hungry pallet with a bigg cup once full, and after that $\frac{1}{2}$ full againe of good pottage.

18.—Tusday. I went to Leigh and gat my bonds in from my Master.

21.—Friday night. I went into old William Hasleden's in Ashton; his wife was sicke and I read in the *Practice of Pietie*,[138] and as I was reading she gave up the ghost.

23.—Lord's day. I went to Wigan, being much disconsolated. Yet the Lord incouragd me, for my hope is in Hime.

27th.—Old Thomas Harison was come over out of Halsall, and his sone and others, amongst whome I was one, went to Jenkins' to drinke, and Mr. Hopwood had sent a letter out of Ouldham to envite me with John Jenkins to his house, and John moved me to goe, soe I was resolved to goe forthwith that night, and it was a hoary, snowy night. But, indeed, the maine reason that movd me to goe this night was because Emm was gone to Chadocke Hall,[139] whome I intended to see, but could not. Soe we came to Manchester about 3 or 4 a clock and with much adoe gat a fire in Fennell streete at one Humphrey Peacocke's, where we stayd till prayers in the church, and then we went to morneing prayer. When it was done we went into a litle old women's house att goeing out of the church, and we bought a puding for a 1d. and a loafe [for] 1d., and eate part and gave the rest to old women, and so parted to Ouldham, where we stayd till Munday, and then came home away by Midleton and over Walkeden Moore,[140] where we ware much disconsolated; but with much trouble of mind and werines of bodie we came home.

JENUERY, 1667

2.—Wedensday. I went to the Funerall of younge John Potter of Lilly Lane, to Winwicke.

6.—Lord's day. Mr. Swift was come to Leigh and sent for me. I owd hime 9 li. and had no monys to pay hime, and I was troubled. But it pleased God that I got 3 li. in readines forthwith, I blesse God, and it gave good content. I was al night with John Chadock and supd with my Master.

24.—Thursday. I went to Warrington and payd some debts I there owd, and att my comeing home was wellcomed with the news of John Greenhoughe's runneing away, which was no litle trouble to me, for I looked upon my selfe even as blasted in the bud, unles the Lord be my helpe, who hath helped me hithertoo and surelie will not now forsake me; for my expectation is Frome hime —3 li.

FEBRUERY, 1667

2.—Saturday morneinge. Thomas Parkinson came to me to write a letter to his wife for hime, for he had beene under the execution of a warrant, and was gotten From his attendencers.

3.—Lord's day. I went with John Potter and Tho. Harison to fatch their wives home From Holland. I was nott att this time mery, for I could not, becaus I lay under sad reproches of persequuteing tongues, such as Tho. Naylor, Glasier, Joshua Naylor, and Mary Rogerson, about the debt of John Greenhough. But I trust in God for aid; He is my refuge. These Himeneus and Philetus and Alexander, as Copersmiths, if not worse, have done me much evill. The Lord reward them.

5.—Tusday. I went to Wigan to Mr. Jolley, who was sole executor for John Greenhough and I movd hime for me, but before I intreated Mr. Earle, curate, his assistance, and I told hime all my mind. I came home better satisfied a great deale.

6.—Wedensday. My Master came to Ashton and some writeings I had to seale which ware seald betweene hime and Raph.

11.—Wedensday. I received that sad sorowfulle newes of Mr. Woods' death, and upon the . . .

[The Diary is imperfect here; the last entry is crossed through, and the remainder of the page is blank, except for the lines:

It's God that fixt my love on onely one,
Whom I'le love till I dye or dye a Nunne.]

MARCH, 1667

28.—Thursday. I went with Constable of Ashton to help hime to gather the Pole mony. I was att this time in a sad, sorowfull estate by reason of my fear of povertie, but O, my soule, cast thy burden upon the Lord; He will sustaine thee. Many be the miserys of the righteous, but the Lord will deliver. Dos not Christ call, Harke: "Come unto me all ye that are weary, and I will give you rest"? Indeed, I must confesse I have a proud envious spirit, seeing and thinkeing of others in theire prosperitie, and am apt to censure God for hard measure unto me. Yet Grudge not to see wicked men prosperous: it's but awhile they shall florish thus; prosperitie will be hard peniworthe for them. Waite thou on God, O my soule, and keape His way. O labour to be content with thy presant condition; God sees it good, it should soe be. O do thou so too labour, O my soule, to bringe thy desires to thy condition, and not thy condition to thy desires.

30.—Lord's day. I went to Winwick with John Potter and dined att Mr. Potter's house.

APRIL, 1667

1.—I went this Munday morneinge to Warington to buy some comodities.

THE DIARY OF ROGER LOWE 113

7.—Lord's day. I went with Sarah Hasleden to Wiggan and heard Bishop preach ... [illegible].

8.—Munday. I was sent for to Leigh by my Master, who had a child interred on this day. Raph Hasleden lent me a horse.

14.—Saturday. I was sadlie unfavoured in my thoughts this morneinge through fear of world, and therefore tooke pen in hand and made these verses followeinge:

> The greifes are many i'th world, I forsee;
> Ah Lord, when wilst Thou come to pitie poor me?
> I'me soe beset with greifes I cannot tell
> Not how to live i'th' world, nor where to dwell.
> But this I'me sure: my hope is fixt in Thee,
> And this joyes me in greatst extremitie.
> Thou wilst not suffer me long t' live in woe;
> Sure, Lord, Thou'le come to visit Thy poor Lowe.
>   Amen. Even soe come Lord Jesus in mercie and
>   not in Justice to me Thy servent.

22.—Lord's day. I went with Thomas Smith and litle John Smith to hear Mr. Gregge, who preacht att John Sutton's, and when we war att Parbridge, by reson it was a rainy day we went to hear Mr. Aspinalle. It was nearer and we all runn home very wett, but John Smith had lost his Gloves, and turned againe From Par Hall and found them.

23.—Munday night. I went to John Robinson's and was all night. After this time I was sadly troubled in my thoughts; but the Lord is my suport.

29th.—Lord's day. I went to hear Mr. Gregge preach att William Turner's in Par. Att afternoone I came home and there was some Leigh persons att Chapelle, and I ingagd them into Tankerfeild's, where I spent 6d. But after theire parteinge a sad disaster befell me, viz., a fallinge out betweene Henry Kenion and me. The after days I made it the lamentation of my private thoughts.

MAY, 1667

1.—Wedensday. Henry Kenion came to Tankerfeild's and sent for [me] and we ware both reconcild, and I was som what joyfull.

2.—Thursday. I went to Warington and payd some mony I there owed. As I came home I intended to call on Mr. Potter, meerely out of love, but he would not goe to take part of 2d. in Beere, but seemed as if he ware angry, Which troubled me very sore. I came home very pensive and sad and not very well.

17.—Friday. I went to Warington and sold Josephus, a booke soe cald *Concerneinge Jewish Warrs*.[141] I was att this time partly ingagd to go to Mr. Harwoode, who lived in Shrowsbury, to live with hime, and he had ingagd one Edw. Bowker de Warington to enquire of my disposition. It troubled me sore.

19.—Lord's day. I went with William Know, William Hasleden, and others into Windle to Cowly Hill to Mrs. Harper's house, and heard Mr. Gregge preach out of these words: "Try all things, but hold all Fast that which is goode."

JUNE, 1667.

2.—Lord's day. I went to Wiggan and dined att James Astleye's, For he would have me to dinner.

9.—Lord's day. I went to one Tickle's house in Sutton with William Knowle and litle John Smith, and heard Mr. Gregge out of these words: "Beware yea of the leaven of the Pharisees, which is hipocresie."

23.—Lord's day. I sat forward with James Jenkins for Chester faire, and when I came there I was scarcely welle; yet it pleased God to inable me so as I did my buisnes very welle.

25th.—Tusday. I came homme.

28.—Friday. I went with William Naylor to Crosson to Mr. Pilkington's man, who owd me Master 30s., but I could not get it. Emme Potter and Eles Taylor was att Halsall; therfore I hasted thither on the

29th day, Saturday, which was 8 miles; came to Halsall and sent for them, and they stayd rather too longe, that I went my selfe downe to old Thomas Harison's, who made much of me and constraind me to stay all night. We went all togather to the Ale house and ware mery, and the next day I came home.

JULY, 1667

9.—Lord's day. I went to James Lowe's on Neawton Comon, where Mr. Baldwin preacht.

10.—Munday. I went to Warington faire and mett Mr. Swift.

15.—Munday. I went to Halsall for to fatch Eles Taylor home, but she could not come with me, soe I lost my labour. Att Ormeskirke I stayd and spent 2d. and went into church and lookd in Earle Darbye's Tombe,[142] and soe came home; onely I cald att Holland att one Corles' house and gave my horse 4d. in Ale.

18.—Thursday. I went to Prescott for to receive 5 li. 10s. of John Walls for Henry Feildinge, but received none. I came away by my brother's, who lived att one Traves' house, near Windleshey Chapelle; stayd diner and soe came home, and att the gate that enters into the further end of Town Feild, comeing from Dock Lane, I found a shoo with a silver claspe in the highway.

20.—Saturday. I went to Halsalle to fatch home Elis Taylor, and mett her att Ormeskirke.

28.—Munday. I went to Warington in compenie with John Potter to Winwick, who was exceedinglie troubled with tooth ach, and James Corles in pullinge it out broke it. Att my comeinge frome Warington I went to Mr. Potter's, and John Potter was laid downe, soe I went to the Schoole and Mr. Jones and I went to the Springe and sent for John Potter, who came. As we came home we cald att Heapie's and there had a hott rye loafe and butter, and I had some suger and nutmeg given me att Warington. I would have a flagon burnt for John, and had.

29.—Tusday. I went to the funerall of Thomas Leech, Inkeaper.

AUGUST, 1667

2.—Tusday. I wente to Neawton faire and to the race with John Potter, but stayd not longe nor was not very merye.

4.—Lord's day. I went with John Jenkins to Standish Church and heard Mr. Bowker preach and dined with hime.

6.—Tusday. I went with William Hasleden to Wiggan to speake to Mr. Earle to mary hime.

THE DIARY OF ROGER LOWE

15.—Thursday. I went to Mr. Walls in Prescott, but did not gat no monys.

18.—Lord's day. I went to see Tom Birchall, who was sicke.

27 August.—Tusday. I went to Prescott againe to Mr. Walls, but he was not att homme.

SEPTEMBER, 1667

8.—Munday. I went to Winwick to Mrs. Potter's Funerall and Elizabeth Taylor rid behind me.

10.—Wedensday. I went to Warington. John Plumpton tooke his leave of Ashton this day, and I parted with hime att Warington bridg very dolefullie. Thomas Peake would gladlie hire me.

13.—Friday. I went to Prescott to Mr. Walls. John Hampson went with me, both about one and the same occasion, but he would not be seene.

18.—Wedensday. I went to Warington and I promised Peake to serve hime 3 yeares for 20 li.

22.—Lord's day. I went to Wiggan, haveing no occasion, but meerely to put of a troubled minde.

23.—Munday. According to my promise I went to Warington to meet Tho. Peake.

29.—Lord's day. I went to John Robinson's and was all night, for they lent me a horse to Chester faire. A very rugged night it was. The other morneinge I hasted away, and it was a very tempestuous morneinge, and in Warington George Chapman gave me 2d. in ale, and behind

Fradsham Hamond overtooke me. I gat to Chester and payd the Londoners, for my intentions was to buy nothinge, and I went to the Castle to see a man condemned to dye—a pretie younge man he was and very sorie I was. I gave a man 2d. in ale to let me admittance into the Castle yard, and he tooke me up and downe. The souldiers was most of them all drunke, and glad I was when I was gotten out of the gates from amongst them.

OCTOBER, 1667

1.—Tusday. I came home, I blesse God, very well, but it was a very stormie and rainie day.

28.—I quitted my selfe of all shop effaires in Ashton, and resigned them over to Thomas Hamond, and ingagd my selfe in Thomas Peake's service. After I came to hime I found his wife of soe crosse a disposition that it put me in a troubled condition, and occasiond me to write theise verses Followinge:

> Int' what strange ragion am I posted now—
> Soe hott a climate as I know not howe
> T'enjoy my selfe, much more to live in peace,
> Unles Jehovah move their tongues to cease.
> The Lord of Hosts, that rules in heaven high,
> Looke downe and help Thy servant mightily;
> Show me such favour as the world may know
> That Thou esteemeth of Thy servant Lowe,
> That such as have no reason, nor yet faith
> May learne to live in peace and not in wrath.
> Lord, if Thou please to show Thy selfe my freind
> I matter not this world for to offend;
> My Saviour dear, in greifes I'le come to Thee:
> There's safe protection in necessitie.
> I live in greifes; I know not where to goe;
> I come to Thee, Lord; shelter Thy poor Lowe.
> Deliverance, I hope, will come ere longe,

And I shall singe not longe the mourner's songe.
Providence sees it good I tossd should be
Upon the waves of worldly miserie,
And tho I be thus fetterd in world's greife,
Providence will att last yeild me releife.
And this I'me sure: my faults have caused this;
Require not then—God doth nothing amisse.
My Soul, Frett not, be patiant but awhile;
That face now frownes will ere long on thee smile,
And though He suffer thee in Keder to dwell
Amongst such blacke mouths as doe yawn like hell,
Yet be assurd, God will preserve thee soe
They may thee scare, they shall not hurt poor Low.
Trust then in God—Hee'le comfort thee in trouble
And answer all thy greifes with care joyes double.
Waite on the Lord, live upright in God's way;
Hee'le rescue out of greifes, Hee'le not longe stay.
Take patiantly the world's affronts—for why?
Because it loves its owne, none will deny;
Aprove thy selfe a stranger to the world's freinds,
For heaven att last to such will make amends.

I had made a peece of a promise to stay three yeares with Mr. Peake, but I found his wife of such a pestilentiall nature that I was weary in a few weekes. In December it pleasd God sorely to visit me with a sad afliction, and longe for the space of nine weekes, after which It pleased God to recover me, and I went againe to Mr. Peake, after many envitations; in which time I sent to Emme my designes and thoughts, enclosed in letters, and in short time made a conclusion of my overtyred thoughts, and upon the 23 March 1668, we consumated our grand designe of mariage att Warington, done by Mr. Ward,[143] minister of Warington, att my Cozen Beckeinson's house. William Eccleston was my good freind. I brought Emme to Neawton, and shee was turned off from her sister and knew not where to Lodge all night. It was her pleasure I should turne backe againe to Warington, which I did with William Eccleston and Henry Heckenbothom, who accompenied us to Neawton.

[The diary breaks off here.]

FEBRUARIE, 1668

1.—Munday. I did nothing, but stayd att home; but was angerd in my mind att Martha Knowle, who had undermind me and gotten a booke out of my hands.

2.—Tusday. I went with Thomas Harrison to Halsall to seale 2 indentures betwixt Thomas Harison and Robert Neale, his aprentice. I went before Thomas, and att Ormeschurch I staid on hime. We stayd till Thursday and soe came home.

6.—Saturday. William Eccleston came to towne and he gave me a quart of ale and enjoined me to goe the Lord's day following to Broad Oake and give Mr. Harye's daughter a note. This day Mr. Jones, Winwick schoole master, sent for me to come to Winwick upon Monday followinge, for his patron, Mr. Leegh,[144] would come and he would make a speech.

7.—Lord's day. I went to Broad Oake. Mr. Gregg preached out 2 Philip. 9, 10.

9.—I went to Winwick and heard Mr. Jones make his speech to Mr. Leegh. I went to Hall Winwick and dind there; after I came with Mr. Watt to the Clarkes' house, and Coz Potter had given Mr. Watt 1d. to spend and I laid another 2d. to it, and when that was drunke I parted.

9.—Tusday. Richard Orme came to Ashton, and I was with John Potter and hime late in Alehouse—which the Lord forgive.

10.—Wedensday. I went to Nicholas Croft's to get in a debt, but gat nothing.

11.—Thursday. I went to Senelly Greene to get a debt oweinge me by Mr. Gerard, Schoole master. Att my returne home I mett with Mr. James Woods comeing out of his unkle's, Raph Lowe's, soe he asked me to goe with them to the Ale house, and I went with them to Tom Hasleden's, and Mr. Woods was very hartie and healthfull. I spent 2d.

[A whole page in the diary is here left blank.]

5.—Lord's day. I received some peece of disgrace in the Chapell from Mr. Atkinson[145] by reason I did not with others stand up att the readinge of the Gospell, but as to the publicke it was litle noted. But I tooke it heineously in my one thoughts by reason I had bespoke my thoughts to hime befor: that I could not conforme to any such Formes; but att after evening prayer I went to hime att Ellins Ashton's and I told hime my mind to the Full: that standing att Gospelle, with other ceremonies now in use, was a meere Romish foperie and I should never doe it; but sith I could not come to the publicke ordinances without publicke disturbance for a ceremoniall faileinge, I should thence forward betake my selfe to such recepticles where I could, to my poor abilitie, serve God without disturbance. Raph Winstanley, Atkinson's deciple of the Blacke tribe of Gad, came in and spoke his venome in a very arogant manner; but I flie to God for refuge.

16.—Munday. I went to Edge Greene to get some mony oweing to me by Nicholas Crouker, but gat none. Cald att Tho. Whitle's, tooke a pipe of tobacco, and then went and bought of Cooper some Ash wood to be two cheares, and brought a peece home with me.

18.—Wedensday. Emme and I went to Warrington and bought some odd things and came home, and was in night; it was a very stormie night. John Low, Blackesmith, let her ride behind hime.

25.—Thursday. I went to Winwick to the Funerall of Dicke Landers. Mr. Potter preached out 10 Job, 20 verse.

MARCH, 1669.

Munday. I went to John Lowe's Smithie to get some odd things made and I went to old John Robbinson to bespeake John Marshe's thoughts to widow Jaxon, old John's daughter, being desired by John Marsh, and shee consented he should come Thursday come seavenight after.

7.—Lord's day. I went to my Cozen Robert Rosbothom and heard Mr. Baldwin preach out 8 Romans, 25, 26 verses.

11.—Thursday. Honest Mr. Hayhurst came to Towne to see me and I was glad to see him.

14.—Lord's day. I went to Leigh to bid a farewelle to poor Mr. Braidley Hayhurst. Mr. Lever preacht out 14 Pro., 9 ver[se]. Att my comeing home I cald on my sister Katherin and advisd her for her good to bethinke her selfe and live godly, consideringe she had but a short time to live here, but she was highly offended, so I came homme, being late in the night.

19.—Friday. I went to the Funeralle of Ellin Potter, daughter to Thomas Potter, and [she] was interred att Winwick. As we came into Winwick churchyard, Captaine Risleye's soldiers ware traineinge, and when we ware att prayers in the church upon the Funeral's occasion the souldiers discharged their musquets three times.

20.—Saturday. I went to Winwick Schoole to get Mr. Jones [to] pay me 30s., but I gat none. This eveninge old Thomas Harison was come over and I spent 2d.

21.—Lord's day. I went For Laverpoole, was all night att my Brother's, and the next day went Forward to Laverpoole; payd Mr. Johnson 5 li. I owd hime.

22 day.—Came home.

27th.—Saturday. I went to Leigh; bought of my Master 9 yards and a ½ of Cersie[146] for a suite of clothes for my selfe.

29.—Munday. I went to Warington, and Mrs. Peake had laid a lye on me about their debts, which occasiond some greife, but I cleard my selfe to her shame.

[MARCH, 1674]

12 March, 1674. I went to Coz Robert Rosbothome to Rixham[147] faire to seeke his mare that was stolne over night, and we mett with Mathew Cooke, who we conjecturd to be the theefe, and upon our wordes he fled and left a stolne mare, which we securd in town and was after ownd ownd [sic].

THE END

NOTES

Abbreviations:
  Baines = Edward Baines, *History of the County Palatine and Duchy of Lancaster*, revised edition by John Harland, 1868–70.
  D.N.B. = *Dictionary of National Biography*.
  V.H.L. = *Victoria History of the County of Lancaster*, edited by William Farrer and J. Brownbill.

[1] He had succeeded James Woods at St. Thomas's Chapel in Ashton in 1663; his Christian name seems to be unknown: *V.H.L.*, IV, 147.

[2] Rainford, Lancs.

[3] Evince.

[4] "On the restoration of the Prayer Book services in 1662 the objectors under the ministry of the ejected curate, James Woods, worshipped in a farm-house": *V.H.L.*, IV, 148. For information regarding the Gaskells see *V.H.L.*, IV, 406.

[5] Golborne, Lancs.

[6] A corruption of the name "Tyldesley Banks."

[7] Knot-grass, or ragwort, so called because it was given to ailing swine.

[8] James Woods, of St. Thomas's Chapel, Ashton; he was in charge of that cure as early as August, 1645. The Commonwealth Church Survey found him to be "a very godly preacher, a man of good life and conversation," appointed "by free election of the whole town." He was ejected in 1662 by the terms of the Act of Uniformity, or Bartholomew Act: *V.H.L.*, IV, 147.

[9] Brynn, one of the ancestral estates of the Gerards, obtained with Ashton and other properties in the hundreds of West Derby and Leyland by the marriage, in the fourteenth century, of William Gerard and Joan, daughter and co-heiress of Alan de Burnhull: *V.H.L.*, IV, 142.

[10] Wigan's importance and wealth in the seventeenth century may be appreciated from its ship-money assessment in 1636: fifty pounds, the highest levy in the county, and twice as much as Liverpool's: Baines, I, 211.

[11] Chowbent, now in Atherton town.

[12] Part of the old Ashton town division of the parish of Ashton-under-Lyne. See *V.H.L.*, IV, 338–9.

[13] He went to Thelwall, Cheshire.

[14] Bent.

[15] Liverpool.

[16] Bamfurlong, in Abram township, Lancs.

[17] Probably Bradley Hayhurst, Vicar of Leigh, from *c.* 1646 to *c.* 1657, when he resigned. In 1661 he was presented to the living of Taxall, Cheshire, where he was probably silenced for nonconformity. In 1661–3 he lived in Manchester; in 1671 he became minister of Macclesfield, resigning in 1682, shortly before he died: *V.H.L.*, III, 419.

[18] Twin.

[19] New Hall, an estate in Ashton acquired in the seventeenth century by the Launder or Lander family.

[20] Dalton, Lancs.

[21] This was the principal mansion of Dalton, and the seat of the Ashurst family. It existed as early as 1649: Baines, II, 186–7. The "most gallant prospect" which Lowe enjoyed was occasioned by Dalton's location upon hilly ground south of the River Douglas, Ashurst Hall lying on the western slope of the ridge: *V.H.L.*, IV, 97.

[22] Whortleberries.

[23] Christopher Love (1618–51) was a militant Presbyterian divine and a prolific writer of sermons, many of which were published. In 1651 Love was found guilty of plotting against the Commonwealth, being charged with corresponding with Charles II and Queen Henrietta Marie; he was executed August 22, 1651. The book which Lowe bought is entitled *Grace: the Truth and Growth and Different Degrees thereof: the Sum and Substance of XV Sermons. Preached by ... Mr. Christopher Love ... They being his Last Sermons. To which is added a Funeral Sermon, being the very Last Sermon He ever Preached*, London, 1652. See *D.N.B.*

[24] Prisoners' base.

[25] Lymm, Cheshire.

[26] Haydock, an ancient manor and township in the parish of Winwick. The local pronunciation is "Haddock": *V.H.L.*, IV, 137.

[27] Probably a hedge-bank, or one of earth thrown up from a ditch.

[28] According to the obituary notes kept by Lowe, Ashton was hanged for murdering a tapster in Nantwich, Cheshire.

[29] These graves cannot now be located.

[30] Complexion.

[31] Abram, Lancs.

[32] Distance, way.

[33] September 22 and 23 were the annual fair-days in Ashton, which doubtless occasioned more than usual merriment: Baines, II, 214.

[34] Leigh, Lancs.

[35] Held, remained.

[36] Godfather.

[37] Possibly William Leigh, Rector of Newchurch, Culcheth,

Lancs., apparently as early as 1645, and afterwards in charge of Gorton Chapel, whence he was ejected in 1662. He was a Fellow of Christ's College, Cambridge. According to Calamy he died of the stone in 1664, aged about fifty. See *V.H.L.*, IV, 165, and Edmund Calamy, *Nonconformist's Memorial* (ed. of Samuel Palmer, 1802–3), II, 363.

[38] Kibbo, stick or cudgel.

[39] Ram.

[40] James Livesey (1625?–82) was Vicar of Great Budworth, Cheshire, from 1657 until his death in 1682. His works show him to have been a man of scholarly abilities. See *D.N.B.*

[41] High Leigh, Cheshire.

[42] Shallow basket.

[43] Making a fuss and noise.

[44] Way, road.

[45] Bottled ale and draught ale.

[46] Hulme, Lancs.

[47] Newton-in-Makerfield, Lancs.

[48] As late as 1836 courts leet and baron were held twice a year at Ashton: *V.H.L.*, IV, 146.

[49] This may refer to Thomas Gregg, ejected from the pulpit of St. Helens Episcopal Chapel in 1662, by the Bartholomew Act. See B. Nightingale, *Lancashire Nonconformity*, IV, 128–9.

[50] Foumart, or polecat, hunting.

[51] Possibly Thomas Blackburne, who ministered at St. Peter's Church, Newton-in-Makerfield, from 1650, coming into the living by the general consent of the chapelry. It may also refer to "Mr. John Blakeburne," mentioned later in the diary: *V.H.L.*, IV, 136.

[52] Possibly the Mr. Bowker whom Lowe refers to as "Vicar of Standish" in his entry for June 27, 1665.

[53] In 1693 the Church of St. Mary the Virgin, Leigh, "possessed four bells said to have been given by Queen Elizabeth, two of which—the great bell and the third bell—had been cast at Leigh in 1663": *V.H.L.*, III, 415.

[54] Course of conduct.

[55] Took care of, attended.

[56] The township of Billinge has long been split into two halves, regarded as separate townships, and known as Chapel End and Higher End. Lowe evidently refers to Chapel End: *V.H.L.*, IV, 83.

[57] Edmund Calamy (1600–66) was an eloquent Presbyterian preacher in London from 1639 till 1662 when, although he had favoured the Restoration, and had been offered the Bishopric of Coventry and Lichfield, he was ejected for nonconformity. He continued, however, to attend the church whence he had been ejected; on December 28, 1662, the preacher not appearing, Calamy was prevailed upon by the congregation to preach, for

NOTES 127

which he was committed to Newgate under the Lord Mayor's warrant—the first of the nonconformists to get into trouble for disobeying the Act of Uniformity. He was liberated, however, by order of the King. He was co-author of the celebrated treatise entitled *Smectymnuus* from the initials of its authors: S. Marshall, E. Calamy, T. Young, M. Newcomen, and W. Spurstowe. His grandson and namesake was the well-known biographer of nonconformity: *D.N.B.*

[58] This was *A Treatise of Prayer and of Divine Providence as relating to it*, published in 1653. Edward Gee (1613-60), minister of Eccleston from 1643 till his death, became a zealous Presbyterian and was active in administering the Presbyterian system in Lancashire. Adam Martindale called him a "great knocker for disputation": *Life*, 91; and see *D.N.B.*

[59] Charles Herle (1598-1659), presented in 1626 to the rich rectory of Winwick by Sir Edward Stanley, was an active and influential Presbyterian, and the most distinguished of Winwick's modern rectors. Frequently a preacher before the Long Parliament, he was one of the twelve divines appointed to license books on divinity, and took a leading part in matters pertaining to Presbyterian organization and doctrine. In 1643 he was President of the Westminster Assembly. He did not reside in Winwick during the war, but returned thither in 1650, and was buried there in 1659. See *D.N.B.*; *V.H.L.*, IV, 128.

[60] Thomas Johnson became Rector of Halsall in 1645: *V.H.L.*, III, 189.

[61] Grappenhall, Cheshire.

[62] Very likely this was Peter Aspinwall, the nonconformist divine who was ejected from Heaton, Lancs., in 1662. He afterwards assumed ministerial duties in Warrington, Lancs., dying there in 1692: Nightingale, *Lancashire Nonconformity*, IV, 213-14.

[63] A collar, lying flat upon the dress, worn by both men and women.

[64] Lately Common, in Bedford township.

[65] Custody, confinement.

[66] A search for vagrants and such petty offenders, carried out by the constables upon the order of the Justices of the Peace.

[67] Thrush.

[68] Piannet, or pianet, a local name for the magpie.

[69] Great Neston, in the hundred of Wirrall, Cheshire.

[70] This hill is supposed to have been the site of a watch-tower: Baines, II, 190.

[71] Blackrod, Lancs.

[72] John Tilsley (1614-84) became Vicar of Dean in 1643. He was described in 1650 as "a painful, godly, preaching minister" and about that time suffered temporary loss of his benefice, owing to his refusal to take the engagement. He assisted in the

formation of the Chetham Library, the founder having nominated him a trustee. He was ejected from Dean Church in 1662, but was allowed to preach there as a lecturer until he was silenced by Bishop Pearson in 1673. He then retired to Manchester, where he died in 1684: *D.N.B.*; *V.H.L.*, V, 4.

[73] John Angier (1605–77) was in charge of Denton Chapel from 1631 until his death, and was one of the most famous Puritans of Lancashire, where he had come in 1629, intending to proceed to New England. Gaining the support of the Hyde and Holland families he was able to remain at Denton after the passing of the Act of Uniformity. He is noted for his dictum against long sermons: "I would rather leave my hearers longing than loathing": *D.N.B.*; *V.H.L.*, IV, 322.

[74] Arsenic.

[75] Remnants.

[76] Apparitor, a summoning officer in an ecclesiastical court.

[77] The Episcopal Chapel of St. Helens was called, according to Halley "St. Mary's by Church folk, but Mary's-in-Ellen's by true Presbyterians": *Lancashire Puritanism and Nonconformity*, II, 320.

[78] Isaac Ambrose (1604–64), a Lancashire nonconformist divine and theological writer. He was, as minister in Preston (1640–54), and in Garstang until ejected in 1662, closely associated with the establishment of Presbyterianism in Lancashire. Called by Halley the most meditative Puritan of Lancashire, he was an advocate of diary-keeping to foster personal piety: *D.N.B.*, and see Introduction above.

[79] George Hall, son of Joseph Hall, Bishop of Norwich, was made Bishop of Chester in 1662. He held the archdeanery of Canterbury and the rectory of Wigan *in commendam*. He died in Wigan in 1668: *D.N.B.*

[80] John Lowe was Vicar of Huyton, succeeding William Bell, ousted in 1662, until his death in 1706. In 1665 he was presented "for not reading divine service as he ought," and for omitting and slighting prayers "to the great displeasure of the parishioners." He was returned as conformable in 1689: *V.H.L.*, III, 155.

[81] Wakes were originally annual festivals kept in commemoration of the completion and dedication of a church, characterized by an all-night watch in the church. The devotional aspect decreased as time went on, and wakes became mere fairs or markets. The Book of Sports of Charles I included wakes among feasts which should be observed.

[82] Overtook [?].

[83] Chowbent, Lancs.

[84] Seneley Green.

[85] Happened to come upon.

NOTES

⁸⁶ The rectory of Winwick. Dr. Kuerden described it in 1695 as "a princely building, equal to the revenue": *V.H.L.*, IV, 123.

⁸⁷ A heifer from one to two years old; sometimes a young bull.

⁸⁸ Probably either Joseph Hanmer, Curate of Ellenbrook, 1664–69? or Samuel Hanmer, his successor.

⁸⁹ Wassail, drinking bout.

⁹⁰ St. Andrew's Day is actually November 30.

⁹¹ Fleam, river.

⁹² Raging.

⁹³ Hearthmen or chimney-men were the collectors of the hated hearth-tax, which existed from 1662 to 1689, when its unpopularity induced the government to abandon it. It was England's only direct tax and amounted to £170,000 annually.

⁹⁴ If Lowe saw any supernatural significance in the comet's appearance, he does not indicate it here. Adam Martindale alludes to this "dreadfull" comet in his diary (p. 179). John Evelyn, an educated man of the world, noting the appearance of a comet in 1680 adds: "We have had of late severall comets, which tho' I believe appeare from naturall causes, and of themselves operate not, yet I cannot despise them. They may be warnings from God, as they commonly are forerunners of his animadversions": *Diary* (Wheatley ed., 1906), II, 380.

⁹⁵ John Lever (1631–92), ejected from Cockey Moor in 1662. "During the time the Nonconformists were outcasts and wanderers, he continued to preach and celebrate the rites of religion as he had opportunity in Bolton and the neighbourhood." After the death of Richard Goodwin in 1685 Lever ministered to the nonconformists in Deansgate. A namesake was then Vicar of Bolton: Nightingale, *Lancashire Nonconformity*, III, 5.

⁹⁶ Played slide-groat or shuffleboard.

⁹⁷ A manor-house in Parr township, once the property of the Parre family, Barons of Kendall. In Lowe's time it was the chief seat of the Byroms: Baines, II, 249.

⁹⁸ Thomas Crompton was minister of the Chapel of St. Stephen, at Astley, consecrated in 1631, from 1632 until his death in 1683. A zealous Presbyterian, ejected for nonconformity in 1662, he remained in charge of the chapel for twenty years thereafter owing to a dispute over the patronage: *V.H.L.*, III, 448–9.

⁹⁹ This is very likely Roger Baldwin, Curate of Eccles, 1646–7, Vicar of Penrith, Cumberland, and after the Restoration, according to Calamy, minister of the nonconformist congregation at Monks' Hall, Eccles: *V.H.L.*, IV, 391.

¹⁰⁰ This refers to Henry Banister of Bank who, according to Lowe's obituary notes "was drawen on a Litter dead through this Town being slaine by Colket att Sir Philip Edgerton att a Race on Forrest of De la Mare." Delamere Forest is in northern Cheshire.

NOTES

[101] England was from 1665 to 1667 engaged in the Second Dutch War. Evelyn notes that April 5, 1665 was "a day of public humiliation and for successe of this terrible war, begun doubtlesse at secret instigation of the French to weaken the States and Protestant interest": *Diary*, II, 179.

[102] The *Autobiography of William Stout*, a Lancashire merchant who lived at the close of the seventeenth century, casts some light on funeral customs of the time. Stout writes: "At this time we sold much cheese to funerals in the country, from 30 lb. to 100 lb. weight, as the deceased was of ability; which was shived into two or three in the lb., and one with a penny manchet [loaf] given to all attendants. And then it was customary, at Lancaster, to give one or two long, called Naples, biscuits, to each attending the funeral": p. 35.

[103] Epilepsy.

[104] James Pilkington was Rector of Croston from 1662 until his death in 1683: Baines, II, 116.

[105] Purged.

[106] Adam Martindale (1623–86), the Presbyterian divine and autobiographer. Ejected from Rosthorne, Cheshire, vicarage in 1662, he was at this time evidently employed as a tutor in the family of Sir Richard Hoghton, of Hoghton Tower. His sister Margaret died in Ashton in 1665: *Life*, 177–9, 186.

[107] Ardent.

[108] A school was founded in Ashton in 1588: *V.H.L.*, IV, 148.

[109] Brother-in-law.

[110] It was caused by a temporary escape of carburetted hydrogen gas.

[111] Ribanding.

[112] A cop is a top of a hill.

[113] Edward Kenyon was Rector of Prestwich from 1660 to 1668. He became a Fellow of St. John's College, Cambridge, where he was educated, in 1653. Appointed before the Restoration "his connections and training would put him on the Presbyterian side, but he seems to have conformed readily to the restoration and the Prayer-book services, and held the rectory till his death": *V.H.L.*, V, 73.

[114] James Jollie (1610–66), known as Major Jollie, was a wealthy clothier. He became Provost-Marshal General for the Parliamentary forces in Lancashire. In 1646 he was nominated an elder for Gorton in the Manchester classis of the Presbyterian organization in Lancashire, but being an independent did not serve: *V.H.L.*, IV, 285; *D.N.B.*

[115] This word has several meanings; it may connote a tinsmith, one who finishes metal goods (in contrast to one who forges them), or, more generally, a worker in metals.

[116] A Gothic building of stone, surrounded by a moat, rebuilt

NOTES 131

in 1616 by Sir Richard Bold. It has since fallen into ruin: Baines, II, 250.

[117] Lodge Hall, an ancient moated manor-house: Baines, II, 202.

[118] The meaning here is probably ale-house. A hot-house can also be a house for hot baths, or a brothel.

[119] Contrived.

[120] September 21.

[121] An instrument of punishment by which a person was made to sit with his ankles secured between two planks, and sometimes his wrists likewise.

[122] Currants.

[123] A cloth, usually of worsted but sometimes of silk, having on one side a velvet nap.

[124] Causey, causeway.

[125] Lowe's only reference to the Civil War. This royalist campaign occurred in July and August, 1648, when an armed force raised by General Sir Marmaduke Langdale in Lancashire and Westmorland was joined to Scottish troops, and the united body, over 20,000 strong, under the command of the Duke of Hamilton, began a march on Manchester. It was intercepted and routed by Cromwell in three battles in three days: Preston, Wigan, and Warrington.

[126] An estate in Bedford township, acquired in the seventeenth century by Sir Henry Sclater: *V.H.L.*, III, 434.

[127] A history of the persecution of reformers in England, by John Foxe, published in 1563. It was entitled *Acts and Monuments*, but popularly known as the *Book of Martyrs*.

[128] Assessed.

[129] Pottle, a two-quart pot or tankard.

[130] Shippen, cow-house or stable.

[131] Frodsham Bridge: it crosses the River Weever at Frodsham, Cheshire.

[132] In 1301 Edward I granted two fairs to John de Langton of Newton Manor, to be held on the eve, day, and morrow of St. John *ante Portam Latinam* (May 6), and of St. Germain (July 31): *V.H.L.*, IV, 135.

[133] The Scholes, a district in Wigan.

[134] Bay, a compartment in a barn.

[135] The manor of Bradley was at this time the property of the Leghs of Lyme. The "fabrick" which Lowe viewed was never reconstructed, and a brick farmhouse was afterwards called Bradley Hall: *V.H.L.*, III, 327.

[136] A seat of the Gerard family in the township of Ashton-in-Makerfield, razed early in the nineteenth century: Baines, II, 214.

[137] Sir William Gerard, who succeeded his father as baronet in 1630. He had been an ardent champion of the royal cause at the

outbreak of the Civil War; appointed Governor of Denbigh Castle, he had sold his Derbyshire estates to help finance the campaign. His estates were consequently sequestrated by Parliament and sold under the confiscatory Act of 1652, but all or most of them were recovered. A contemporary letter describes Sir William as a "subtle jesuited Papist": *V.H.L.*, IV, 145.

[138] *The Practice of Piety* was written by Lewis Bayly, Bishop of Bangor, and constitutes his chief claim to fame. The date of its first publication is unknown, but by 1613 it had reached its third edition. Its popularity in Puritan circles knew no bounds: in 1735 it was in its fifty-ninth edition and had been translated into many foreign tongues, including the language of the Indians living around Cambridge, Massachusetts. Bunyan ascribes to it his first spiritual experiences: *D.N.B.*

[139] Located in the township of Tyldesley, Lancs.

[140] A desolate region in winter at this time. The Eccles parish register records the burial of a man who had perished in crossing it.

[141] Flavius Josephus' *The Jewish War*, the oldest of his extant works, written near the end of Vespasian's reign (69–79).

[142] The Church of St. Peter and St. Paul in Ormskirk, said to have been established by one Orm in 1068, contains the Derby Chapel, with the family vault, constructed in 1572 by Edward ("the Bountiful"), third Earl of Derby.

[143] Joseph Ward, Rector of Warrington from 1664 till 1691. He was listed as conformable in 1689: *V.H.L.*, III, 312.

[144] Piers Legh, Esq., of Lyme. The school was founded in the reign of Henry VIII by Gowther Legh, and refounded by Sir Peter Legh in 1619: *V.H.L.*, IV, 130.

[145] He succeeded Mr. Maddock as Vicar of Ashton in 1668: *V.H.L.*, IV, 147.

[146] Kersey, a kind of coarse narrow woollen cloth, usually ribbed.

[147] Rixton [?].

APPENDIX

ROGER LOWE seems to have been taken ill early in 1679, and to have died without making a will. Administration of his property was granted to Emma Lowe, his widow, and an inventory, preserved in the Probate Court at Chester, was taken April 22, 1679. The administration and inventory read:

Roger Lowe, late of Ashton, husbandman; administration to Emma Lowe, widdow, the relict, 5 May 1679.

The 22 Aprill 1679. A true and perfect inventory of all the goods, cattels, chattels, debts, and rights of Roger Lowe, late of Ashton, late deceased, apprised and valued by us, Matthew Deane, John Potter, Thomas Harrison, and Willm Lowe.

	li.	s.	d.
Imprimis, two milke cowes at	6	0	0
Item, one presse in the loft over the house	0	8	0
Item, one long table in the said loft	0	10	0
Item, 6 cheeres in the said loft	0	16	0
Item, one table cloth	0	1	0
Item, 3 chusshions	0	2	0
Item, one bedstead in the roome over the shop, 2 featherbeds, 2 feather boulsters, one chaffe boulster, three feather pillowes, 2 coverlids, and 2 blankitts, at	3	0	0
Item, one arke in the said roome	0	10	0
Item, one truncke	0	4	0
Item, 3 tresses, 2 boxes, 2 cowfors,* and 4 chusshions	0	9	0

* Coffers.

Item, one bedstead and bedding in the chamber as it now stands	1	10	0
Item, one cubboard in the house	1	0	0
Item, one settle in the house	0	6	0
Item, one little table, 2 cheeres, fall board, backestoole	0	5	0
Item, one clocke weights and case	1	10	0
Item, one close stoole, 2 looking glasses	0	3	0
Item, one backestone, 2 iron grates, and other iron geere	1	0	0
Item, one churne and other treene ware	0	10	0
Item, in earthen vessels	0	2	0
Item, 4 dosin of trenchers	0	3	0
Item, one white plate	0	1	0
Item, in pewter	1	16	0
Item, in brasse	1	11	0
Item, in linnen	2	0	0
Item, two bedsteads and one table	1	6	0
Item, for goods beinge in the shop*.	29	3	0
Item, in moneyes oweinge by severall persons in the debt booke	6	0	0
Suma tot	60	6	4

Apprised by
Matthew Deane
John Potter
Thomas Harrison
Willm. Lowe

* Indicating that Lowe remained a trader all his days.

INDEX

Abram, 34, 103, 109
Accounts, reckoning of, 21, 26, 46, 52, 60, 62, 67, 69, 76, 80, 87, 93
Ale, accommodation with, 45–6; bottled and common, 41; jelly-bowl of, 34; roseberry, 106
Ambrose, Isaac, 67, 101
Angier, John, 63
Apparitor, 66
Apprentice, runaway, 56, 111
Apprenticeship, ending of, 26; of a drunken youth, 53
Apprenticing, 74, 88
Ashton, Hamblett, 29
Ashton-in-Makerfield, chapel, 51; court, 44; school, 84, 104; schoolmaster, 84, 104; Town Field, 22, 27–8, 48, 58, 85, 96, 116; Town Green, 85; Town Heath, 15–7, 28, 53, 55, 59, 64; Vicars of, 13, 121
Ashurst Hall, 23
Assizes, 69–71
Astley, 18
Atheism, sermon against, 105
Atherton, 78, 87, 99
Atkinson, —, Vicar of Ashton, 121

Baldwin, Roger(?), 82, 115, 122
Bamfurlong, 20–4, 26, 29, 41–4, 46, 48, 51, 56, 60–2, 64, 67, 72, 75–6, 78–80, 84, 86, 104
Banister, Henry, 82
Barrow, Anne, 13–4, 25, 33–4, 42–8, 52–3, 88

Battersbie, John, 14
Beer, spiced, 46
Bell, tolling, 72
Bells, casting of Leigh, 46
Berry-picking, 23
Best man, Lowe a, 82
Betting, 36
Billinge, 63; Chapel, 50, 62, 90, 92, 97, 103, 106, 108
Birds' nests, hunting, 59, 62
Bishop of Chester, 67, 72, 105–7, 113
Bishop's Court, 59
Blackly Hurst, 79, 103
Blackrod, 63
Blakeburne, —, 45, 103, 106–7, John, 92, 98, 108–9
Blood, verse for staunching, 77
Bold Hall, 87
Bolton, 62
Bonds, making, 58, 72–3, 87
Book of Martyrs 99
Bowker, —, 82, 84, 87, 96–7, 104, 116
Bowling, 28, 33, 86, 88–9, 103
Bradley Hall, 107
Broad Oak, 120
Brothers, references to Lowe's, 14, 23, 37, 44, 61–2, 73–4, 83, 99, 123
Brynn, 16, 34, 104
Budworth, Cheshire, 39
Burning well, 85
Burton Wood, 107
Byrom family, 58, 81, 84

Callamy, Edmund, 50
Candles, purchase of, 66
Carr Mill, 74
Castle Hill, 63

INDEX

Chadocke, John, 18, 21–2, 36, 49–50, 57, 59–60, 65, 71, 74, 81, 85, 105, 108, 110
Chadocke Hall, 110
Cheshire, 18, 25, 35
Chester, 28–9, 47, 87, 100, 103–4, 118; Castle, 118; Fair, 36, 61, 86, 115, 117
Child-birth, 73, 93, 97, 100
Choristers, 94, 104
Chorley, 106; Moor, 106
Chowbent, 17, 71, 79, 87–8
Christenings, 26, 74–5, 78, 96–7
Clothing, 18, 20, 50, 61, 65, 95, 123
Coal-pits, 57
Cock-fight, 105
Comet, 77
Communion, 44, 78, 90
Constables, 69, 112
Cowley Hill, 61, 114
Crompton, Thomas, 81
Croston, 83, 106, 115

Daisy Hillock, 83, 99
Dalton, 23, 55
Dame, Lowe's, 24, 50–1, 57, 64–5, 85
Dean Church, 63, 71
Debts, collecting, 27–8, 37, 67, 91, 106, 114, 117, 121, 123; paying, 99–100, 106, 108, 110–1, 123
Delamere Forest, 82
Denton Green, 88, 91
Derby, tomb of Earl of, 115
Dock Lane, 28, 69–70, 116
"Dragon" (Chester), 104
Drink, spiced, 49
Drunkenness, 118

Earle, —, 111, 116
Eccleston, 54; Church, 54
Edge Green, 22, 47, 55, 79, 88, 121
Episcopacy and presbytery, discourses on, 52, 67, 89

Feebleness, after illness, 101, 103
Fire, 107; of London, 108
Fishing, 23
Foumart-hunting, 44
Frodsham, Cheshire, 118; Bridge, 104
Funerals, 16, 20, 26, 64, 66, 70–1, 76, 78–9, 82, 89, 96–7, 99, 107, 109–10, 113, 116–7, 122; refreshment at, 109

Garswood, 108
Gaskell, Lawrence, 13
Gee, Edward, 54
Gerard, Sir William, 99, 108
Godfather, 35, 71, 80; Lowe, a, 96
Golborne, 14, 27, 43, 45, 47–8, 56, 69, 79; Cop, 85–6, 89, 97; stocks, 27
Goose Green, 58, 90
Grappenhall Church, Cheshire, 57
Graves, looking at, 57, 77
Greensworth, Anne, 20, 24, 27, 29, 41, 46, 51, 56, 59, 62, 65, 76, 80, 86; Robert, 73, 80, 87
Gregg, Thomas(?), 44, 61, 113–5

Hall, Dr. George (Bishop of Chester), 67, 72, 105–7, 113
Halsall, 54, 84, 110, 115–6, 120
Hamilton, Duke of, 96
Harvesting, 34
Hasleden, John, 13, 16, 19, 34, 36, 38, 40–3, 49, 52–3, 55–9, 67, 71, 73, 75, 77–8, 81–3, 88
Haydock, 26, 29, 33, 40, 69, 91; Wood, 95
Hayhurst, Bradley, 21, 122
Hearthman, visit of, 77
Heifer, purchase of, 81

INDEX

Hen and chickens, purchase of, 42
Herle, Charles, 54
High Leigh, Cheshire, 39
Hindley, 63, 67, 78
Holland, Lancashire, 23, 45, 50, 82, 96, 111, 115
Horse, loan of a, 104, 113, 117; theft of a, 123
Horse-head-under-Bank Field, 83
Horse-race, 27
Horseshoe Field, 59
Houghton, 63, 79, 83; Chapel, 79; Common, 63
Hour-glasses, purchase of, 60
Hulme, 43
Hunting, 95
Hurst Ground, 58
Huyton, 67, 100

Illnesses, Lowe's, 22, 28, 41–2, 44, 52, 56, 62, 66, 75, 81, 99–101, 115, 119
Indentures, making, 67, 87; sealing, 120

Jewish War, The, 114
Johnson, Thomas, 54
Jollie, Major James, 87
Jones, —, Winwick Schoolmaster, 120, 123
Josephus, Flavius, 114
Journeyman, Lowe sought as, 93

Kenyon, Edward, 86
Kersey, 123
King's Navy, 82
Knowsley, 107

Lancashire, Under-Sheriff of, 73
Latchford Heath, Cheshire, 25, 57
Lately Common, 57
Lawsuit, 44

Lealand, Alice, 20, 27, 29, 35
Lease, making a, 81
Leigh —, Ashton schoolmaster, 84; Piers, 120: William, 38–9
Leigh, 14, 16, 18, 22, 24, 26, 28–9, 34–6, 38, 46, 48–50, 52, 57, 59–60, 63, 65–6, 69, 71–4, 77, 81, 83, 85–8, 90, 92–5, 98–100, 105, 108–10, 113, 122–3; bells, 46; Church, 58; exercise, 55; schoolmaster, 14, 77; stocks, 92
Lemon, 54
Letter-writing, for others, 24, 28, 42–3, 46, 48, 51, 53, 62–3
Lever, John, 79, 122
Light Oaks, 98
Lilly Lane, 53, 78, 110
Liver, receipt for diseased, 17
Liverpool, 19, 91, 93, 99, 123
Livesey, James, 39
Loaf, 110, 116
Lodge, Chowbent, 87
London, fire of, 108
Love, Christopher, 25
Love-letter, found, 56; writing a, 43
Low, Hugh, 14
Lowe, John, 67, 100; Roger, in wedding party, 13, 49–50; 82; as mediator, 14–5, adopted "son and twindle," 21; visit to Ashurst Hall, 23; visits Mr. Woods in Thelwall, Cheshire, 25, 57; in horse-race, 27; visits parents' graves, 29, 77; becomes master's son's teacher, 37, sues in Ashton court, 44; visits coal-pits, 57; visits woman accused of infanticide, 58; accompanies constable during private

INDEX

search, 59; controversies on religion, 52, 64, 67, 89; visits St. Helen's Chapel, 66; hears Bishop of Chester, 67, 72, 105, 113; a godfather, 74; sees comet, 77; attends funeral of brother's child, 78; visits burning well, Pemberton, 85; at Liverpool, 91, 99, 123; becomes free, 92–3; at Manchester, 94, 110; death of sister, 97; at Chester, 104, 115, 118; sees cock-fight, 105; at Bradley Hall, 107; at Chester Fair, 115; at Warrington Fair, 115; retires from trade in Ashton, 118; enters service of Thomas Peake, 118; marries Emma Potter, 119; quarrel with Vicar of Ashton, 121
Lowton, 69; Common, 90
Lymm, Cheshire, 25, 57

Madocke, —, Vicar of Ashton, 13
Manchester, 94, 110
Mare, a stolen, 123
Marl-pit, 61
Marriage, Lowe's, 119
Martindale, Adam, 84, 87
Master, references to Lowe's, 16, 18, 19–20, 28, 36–7, 43, 49–52, 60–1, 70, 73–6, 81, 83–8, 91–3, 96, 98, 105, 108–11, 113, 115, 123
Match-making, 73–4, 87
Middleton, 110
Moss Side, 18
Music, 45, 94, 104

Navy, 82
Naylor, Mary, 20–8, 34–8, 41–3, 45–7, 61–3
Nephew, named Roger, 97

New Hall, 22
Newton-in-Makerfield, 25, 33, 37, 43, 68, 70, 78, 86, 89, 92, 96, 99, 109, 119–20; Common, 44, 115; Fair, 105, 116
Night-hooks, 62
Nutmeg, 116

Observation, 64
Oldham, 110
Organs, 16, 104
Ormskirk, 115–6, 120
Orrell Moor, 84

Papists, 64, 66, 82
Park Lane, 51
Parr Bridge, 113; Hall, 81, 113
Peake, Thomas, 57, 93, 117–9; Mrs. Thomas, 118–9, 123
Pemberton, 46, 58, 85; burning well at, 85
Philanthropy, 108
Pilkington, James, 83, 106, 115
Platt Bridge, 67
Plums, 27
Poetry by Lowe, 33, 35, 54, 80, 112–3
Poll-money, 112
Pottage, 39
Potter, Emma, 45, 58, 64, 68, 70, 72, 79, 84, 90, 97, 99, 103, 105–7, 110, 115, 119, 122
Practice of Piety, 109
Prayer, 15–6, 42, 44, 51, 53–5, 58–9, 100, 110; evening, 67; private day of, 18, 90
Prescot, 73–4, 106, 116–7
Presentments for assizes, 69–70
Preston, 101, 104
Prestwich, 86
Prisoners' base, 25
Psalm-singing, 15, 28–9, 36, 44
Pudding, 110

Race, 34, 116

INDEX

Rainford, 13, 59, 78, 82–3
Receipt for diseased liver, 17
Religion, argument on, 94, 97
Ribbon, 50
Risley, Captain, 122
Robbery, 36
Roseberry, ale, 106

Sacrament, 78, 90–1
St. Helen's, 78; Chapel, 66
Sankey Hall, 66, 70
Scholes, 106
Scofield, William, 37
Scott, Ellen, 23, 42, 45, 51, 56, 58, 75
Scythe-stones, purchase of, 63, 87
Search, private, 59
Seneley Green, 71, 121
Sermons, 19, 44, 57, 61, 67, 78, 81–2, 86–8, 90, 105–7, 109, 114–5, 120, 122; repetition of, 16, 20, 51, 88; writing of, 51, 58
Sheets, foul, 94
Shooting, 60
Show, 106
Shrewsbury, 114
Shuffleboard, 79
Sisters, Lowe's: Ellen, 52, 55, 59, 74, 77, 95, 97; death of Ellen, 97; Katherine, 52, 122
Skull, 96
Slate Fields, 81
Slater, Sir William, 98–9
Soldiers, drunken, 118; training, 122–3
Standish, 82, 87, 95, 104; Church, 116
Staunching blood, verse for, 77
Stocks, 92
Sugar, 116
Suicide, 100
Sutton, 115

Taylor, Lucy, 70
Teaching, 37, 53

Thelwall, Cheshire, 25, 57
Tilsley, John, 63
Tobacco, 44, 61, 121
Tooth, extraction of a, 116
Tup, adventure with a, 38
Twist, purchase of, 75
Tyldesley Banks, 14

Under-Sheriff of Lancashire, 73

Vicar's Field, Leigh, 29

Wakefield, Yorkshire, 54, 57
Walkden Moor, 110
Ward, Joseph, 119
Warrington, 18–9, 23, 25, 29, 37, 43, 47, 57, 64, 66, 73, 86, 89, 93, 96, 99, 104, 106–7, 111–2, 114; Bridge, 117; Fair, 48, 115
Wassail, 75
Wax, purchase of, 69, 71
Weddings, 13, 49–50, 82; Lowe's wedding, 119
West Leigh, 49; Heath, 59
Whitesmiths, 87
Whitleigh Green, 19, 28, 76, 85, 101, 103
Wigan, 16, 20–1, 27, 35, 50, 63, 67, 71–2, 74–6, 82, 86, 88, 90, 95, 105–7, 109, 111, 113–4, 116–7
Wills, drawing, 19, 62
Windle, 23, 61, 71, 74, 78–9, 83, 88
Wine, 68
Winwick, 16, 20, 26, 34, 54, 64, 66, 70–3, 75, 78–80, 82, 89, 91, 96–9, 103, 107–10, 112, 116–7, 120, 122; Hall, 73, 120; school, 120, 123; Schoolmaster, 120, 123
Woods, James, 15–9, 22, 25–6, 29, 35, 43–4, 49–51, 55, 57–8, 69, 77, 81, 84, 90, 95, 99; death of, 111

York, 75
Yorkshire, 26